Why Do You Need This New Edition?

If you're wondering why you need this third edition of *Principles of Writing Research Papers,* here are 5 good reasons:

1 Coverage of MLA style has been thoroughly updated to reflect the newest guidelines, so you can cite sources confidently.

2 **Expanded strategies and advice for avoiding plagiarism** help you avoid the traps of "unintentional plagiarism."

3 **Updated coverage about using databases** provides accurate and useful information to help you go beyond a general Internet search and find credible, authoritative sources.

4 **New examples, research proposals, and research papers** show you what the final product should look like, whether you are using MLA style to document and format your research project.

5 **Updated coverage of online research strategies** helps you select the most relevant Internet search engines, including detailed advice on where to find respected scholarly sources.

about the authors

PROFESSOR J. D. LESTER
(1935–2006) was a distinguished scholar
of literature and mythology who taught
for 30 years at Austin Peay State
University in Clarksville, Tennessee.
With over 33 published books to his
credit, he continues to be best known
for his hallmark research textbook,
*Writing Research Papers: A Complete
Guide.* Now in its thirteenth edition, this best-selling text has been
used and praised by nearly three million students and instructors alike.

JAMES D. LESTER, JR. is an
instructor of composition at Austin
Peay State University in Clarksville,
Tennessee. His 28 years of experience
as a classroom teacher at both the
college and high school levels have
helped him to create a practical and
manageable guide to direct learners
through the research process. Professor
Lester earned his Ph.D. in English Education from Georgia State
University in Atlanta, Georgia.

PENGUIN ACADEMICS

PRINCIPLES OF WRITING RESEARCH PAPERS

THIRD EDITION

James D. Lester

James D. Lester, Jr.
Austin Peay State University

Longman

Boston   Columbus   Indianapolis   New York   San Francisco
Upper Saddle River   Amsterdam   Cape Town   Dubai   London   Madrid
Milan   Munich   Paris   Montreal   Toronto   Delhi   Mexico City
São Paulo   Sydney   Hong Kong   Seoul   Singapore   Taipei   Tokyo

Senior Sponsoring Editor: Virginia L. Blanford
Senior Marketing Manager: Susan Stoudt
Production Manager: Savoula Amanatidis
Project Coordination, Text Design, and Electronic Page Makeup: Electronic Publishing
    Services Inc., NYC
Cover Design Manager: Nancy Danahy
Senior Manufacturing Buyer: Roy L. Pickering, Jr.
Printer and Binder: Courier Corporation–Westford
Cover Printer: Lehigh-Phoenix Color Corporation

Library of Congress Cataloging-in-Publication Data
Lester, James D., 1935–2006
    Principles of writing research papers / James D. Lester and James D. Lester, Jr.—
    3rd ed.
        p. cm.
    Includes bibliographical references and index.
    ISBN 978-0-205-79182-8
    1. Report writing—Handbooks, manuals, etc. 2. Research—Handbooks, manuals,
etc. I. Lester, James D. II. Lester, James D., 1959– III. Title.
LB2369.L393 2011
808'.02—dc22   2009047523

For more information about the Penguin Academics series, please contact us by mail
at Pearson Education, attn: Marketing Department, 51 Madison Avenue, 29th Floor,
New York, NY 10010, or visit us online at www.pearsonhighered.com/english.

Please visit us at www.pearsonhighered.com.

Longman
is an imprint of

2 3 4 5 6 7 8 9 10—CW—13 12 11 10

ISBN-13: 978-0-205-79182-8
ISBN-10:   0-205-79182-4

detailed contents

| CHAPTER 8 | Writing Effective Notes 91

| CHAPTER 9 | Drafting the Paper in an Academic Style 110

preface

Principles of Writing Research Papers is designed as a brief, inexpensive guide for students writing research papers in both first-year writing courses and upper-level courses that rely on the style guidelines of the Modern Language Association. Since MLA has recently significantly rewritten their style guidelines (*MLA Style Manual*, 3rd edition, 2008 and *MLA Handbook for Writers of Research Papers*, 7th edition, 2009), this guide has also been significantly revised in this edition.

What's New in This Edition

The primary change is, of course, the incorporation of the new MLA citation guidelines, particularly in Chapters 10 and 11. Chapter 12, on preparing electronic research projects, is also revised and updated significantly to reflect the current state of electronic publishing. The organization has also been revised to place the chapter on plagiarism earlier in the text, immediately following the chapters on finding sources, and to emphasize the critical importance of this topic in the writing process.

What This Book Includes

As part of its mission to offer clear, comprehensive guidance for students engaged in writing research papers, this guide offers:

- **An emphasis on academic integrity.** Electronic retrieval has made plagiarism a pervasive problem. Our brief, to-the-point chapter on using sources appropriately defines plagiarism clearly, and a repeated sample passage demonstrates the difference between writing that cites sources properly and writing that fails the test of plagiarism in both obvious and subtle ways.
- **Well-focused information on electronic research.** This text spotlights the academic databases that can be accessed only through a library's

electronic system. It encourages controlled Internet searches and sets guidelines for acceptable academic sites. It helps students conduct field research by providing information about interviews, questionnaires, and correspondence by e-mail, text message, and Web conferencing. And it offers a comprehensive list by discipline of important reference search engines and tools.

- **A thorough discussion of composing from sources.** *Principles* helps students find good sources, create effective notes in a variety of ways, and then—most important of all—blend those sources into an effective piece of writing, one in which the student's voice is not lost, yet in which the sources provide support and confirmation of key concepts and theories.

- **Comprehensive information about documenting with MLA style.** The default style for textual instruction in this book is the MLA style that is typically followed in literature and composition courses. Hence, our guidelines conform to those in the *MLA Handbook*, 7th edition (2009).

- **Help with electronic presentation of research.** *Principles* has a complete chapter for students who wish to present their research in a form other than print. The chapter explains various methods for developing presentations including PowerPoint slides, Web sites, and digital graphics, and provides support for delivering papers and projects electronically.

- **Student papers as models.** Three student papers offer models for students who are preparing their own research papers.

Acknowledgments

Heartfelt appreciation is extended to the members of our family: Martha, Mark, Caleb, Sarah, Whitney, and Peyton, and to our editors and friends at Pearson Longman. Their love and patience made this project possible.

James D. Lester, Jr.
james.lester@cmcss.net

CHAPTER 1

Writing from Research

Communication begins when we make an initial choice to speak or to record our ideas in writing. When we speak, our words disappear quickly, so we are often lax about our grammar since no record of what we say remains. The written word, however, creates a public record of our knowledge, our opinions, and our skill with language, so we try to make our writing accurate, forceful, and honest. A piece of writing—whether it is a history paper, a field report, or a research project—commits our personal concerns to public knowledge.

Regardless of the writer's experience or the instructor's expert direction, writing is a demanding process that requires commitment. Discovering a well-focused topic, and more importantly a reason for writing about it, begins the process. Choosing a format, exploring sources through critical reading, and then completing the writing task with grace and style are daunting tasks.

Writing is an outlet for the inquisitive and creative nature in each of us. Our writing is affected by the richness of our language, by our background and experiences, by our targeted audience, and by the form of expression that we choose. With perceptive enthusiasm for relating detailed concepts and honest insights, we discover the power of our own words. The satisfaction of writing well and relating our understanding to others provides intellectual stimulation and insight into our own beliefs and values.

As a college student, you will find that your writing assignments extend past personal thoughts and ideas to explore more complex aspects of academic studies. This exploration will make you confident in your ability to find information and present it effectively in all kinds of ways and for all sorts of projects:

- A theme in a first-year composition course on the value of Web logs, online journals, and other online discussion groups
- A history paper on Herbert Hoover's ineffectual policies for coping with the Great Depression of the early 1930s
- A report for a physical fitness class on the benefits of ballroom dancing as exercise
- A sociological field report on free and reduced lunches for school-aged children
- A brief biographical study of a famous person, such as labor leader César Chávez

All of these papers require some type of "researched writing." Papers similar to these will appear on your schedule during the first few years of your college career and will increase in frequency in upper-division courses.

Each classroom and each instructor will make different demands on your talents, yet all will stipulate *researched writing*. Your research project will advance your theme and provide convincing proof for your inquiry.

- *Researched writing* grows from investigation.
- *Researched writing* establishes a clear purpose.
- *Researched writing* develops analysis for a variety of topics.

With the guidance of your instructor, you will make inquiry to advance your own knowledge as well as the data for future research by others.

1a Generating Ideas and Focusing the Subject

You can generate ideas for research and focus on the issues with a number of techniques.

- Relate your personal experiences to scholarly problems and academic disciplines.
- Speculate about the subject by listing issues, asking questions, engaging in free writing, talking with others, and using other idea-generating ideas.
- Examine online sources.
- Read textbooks and reference books.

Relate Your Personal Ideas to a Scholarly Problem

Draw on yourself for ideas, keep a research journal, ask yourself questions, and get comfortable with new terminology. Contemplate personal issues to generate ideas worthy of investigation. At a quiet time, begin writing, questioning, and pushing on the various buttons of your mind for your feelings and attitudes. Your research paper should reflect your thinking in response to the sources. It should not merely report what others have said. If possible, combine a personal interest with one aspect of your academic studies:

PERSONAL INTEREST:	Skiing
ACADEMIC SUBJECT:	Sports Medicine
POSSIBLE TOPICS:	"Protecting the Knees"
	"Therapy for Strained Muscles"
	"Skin Treatments"

You might also consider social issues that affect you and your family:

PERSONAL INTEREST:	The behavior of my child in school
ACADEMIC SUBJECT:	Education
POSSIBLE TOPICS:	"Children Who Are Hyperactive"
	"Should School Children Take Medicine to Calm Their Hyperactivity?"

Your cultural background can prompt you toward detailed research into your roots, your culture, and the mythology and history of your ethnic background:

ACADEMIC SUBJECT:	History
ETHNIC BACKGROUND:	Hispanic
PERSONAL INTEREST:	Struggles of the Hispanic child in an American classroom
POSSIBLE TOPIC:	"Bicultural Experiences of Hispanic Students: The Failures and Triumphs"

Developing a Research Journal

Unlike a diary of personal thoughts about your daily activities or a journal of creative ideas, such as poems, stories, or scenarios, the **research journal** enables you to list issues, raise questions, create notes, and develop pieces of free writing. The research journal can be created in a handwritten notebook or as a document file on your personal computer.

You should build the journal primarily with **free writing** as well as **key words and phrases** that come to mind. These establish primary categories for your research. One student listed several terms and phrases about the use of midwives in the rural Southeastern mountains:

natural childbirth	disinfectants	recovery time
prenatal care	medicines	delivery
hardships	complications	sterilization
delivery problems	deaths	cost

In her research journal she began writing notes on the various topics, such as this one:

> The cost of delivery by a midwife in the mother's home differs so greatly from the cost of a doctor and a hospital that we can only appreciate the plight of those using this procedure.

The research journal also provides a place for preliminary outlining to find the major and minor issues, as shown here:

Midwives in the Rural Southeast Mountains

Preparation:	Delivery:	Recovery:	Cost:
prenatal care	natural childbirth	after delivery	one fee
sterilization	medicines	recovery time	
disinfectants	delivery techniques	deaths	

Asking Questions

Asking questions in your research journal can focus your attention on primary issues, and your subsequent notes to answer the questions can launch your investigation. For example, having read Henry Thoreau's essay "Civil Disobedience," one writer posed these questions:

What is "civil disobedience"?
Is dissent legal? Is it moral? Is it patriotic?
Is dissent a liberal activity? Conservative?
Should the government encourage or stifle dissent?
Is passive resistance effective?

Answering the questions can lead the writer to a central issue or argument, such as "Civil Disobedience: Shaping Our Nation."

Academic disciplines across the curriculum invite questions that might provoke a variety of answers and give focus to the subject, as with "sports gambling."

ECONOMICS:	Does sports gambling benefit a college's athletic budget? Does it benefit the national economy?
PSYCHOLOGY:	What is the effect of gambling on the mental attitude of the college athlete who knows that huge sums hang in the balance on his or her performance?
HISTORY:	Does gambling on sporting events have an identifiable tradition?
SOCIOLOGY:	What compulsion in human nature prompts people to gamble on athletic prowess?
POLITICAL SCIENCE:	What laws exist in this state for the control of illegal sports gambling? Are they enforced?

Using Key Terminology

Each discipline has its own terminology. For example, in researching a paper on retail marketing you might learn to refer to "the demographics" of a "target audience." In psychological research you might learn to use the phrases "control group" and "experimental group." One student found essential words for her paper on diabetes:

diabetes	diabetes mellitus	glucose
insulin	metabolize	hyperglycemia
pancreas	ketacidosis	ketones

She learned the meaning of each term and applied them properly in her paper, giving her work a scholarly edge.

Talking with Others to Find and Refine the Topic

Sometime early in your project, go outside yourself to get feedback on your possible topic and its issues. You can accomplish this task by personally interviewing appropriate people and participating in online discussion groups.

Personal Interviews

A personal interview, whether conducted face to face, by telephone, or by e-mail, allows you to consult with experts and people in your community for ideas and reactions to your subject. Explore a subject for key ideas while having coffee or a soda with a colleague, relative, or work associate.

> **HINT**
>
> Casual conversations which contribute to your understanding of the subject need not be documented. However, a formal interview or an in-depth discussion with an expert will demand credit in your text and a citation in the Works Cited page at the end of your paper.

Online Discussion Groups

What are other people saying about your subject? You might use the computer to share ideas and messages with other scholars interested in your subject. Somebody may answer a question or point to an interesting aspect which has not occurred to you. With discussion groups you have a choice:

- Classroom e-mail groups that participate in online discussions of various issues
- Online courses that feature a discussion room
- Real-time chatting with participants online at the same time, in some cases with audio and video

During an online chat conversation, you might find a few ideas on your topic; however, *heed this warning*: participants may use fictitious names, provide unreliable sources, and be highly opinionated in most instances, and therefore *they cannot be quoted in your paper*. The best you might gain is marginal insight into the ideas of people who are often eccentric and who hide behind their anonymity.

Using Electronic Sources

The Internet provides a quick and easy way to find a topic and to refine it to academic standards; however, do not neglect the library's academic databases and its electronic book catalog.

Internet Keyword Search

Articles on the Internet offer ideas about how other people approach the subject, and these ideas can help you refine your topic. Use the subject directory in a search engine, such as Google.com, to probe from a general topic to specific articles (Health > Diseases > Blood disorders > Anemia). Use a keyword search when you already have a specific topic. Thus, entering the word *anemia* will send you immediately to various Web articles. See Chapter 3, pages 38–51, for searching the Internet.

Library Databases

Go to the reliable databases available through your library, such as InfoTrac, UMI ProQuest, or EBSCOhost. You can reach these from remote locations at home or the dorm room by connecting to your library with your personal identification number. The library has monitored Internet sites filtered by editorial boards and peer review. Many articles on these databases have appeared first in print. In many cases you can read an abstract of the article before reading the full text. You can also print the article without going into the stacks. However, libraries vary in their access to electronic databases, so be sure to consult with the reference librarians before attempting to access databases.

Electronic Resources Catalog

Use your library's computerized index to find books, films, DVD holdings, and similar items. Enter a keyword term or phrase, such as *Nancy Pelosi*, and you will get a listing of all relevant books by and about the first woman speaker of the house. The book catalog will not index the titles to articles in magazines and journals, but it will tell you which periodicals are housed in the library and whether they are housed in a printed volume, on microforms, or in an electronic database (see immediately above). Instructors will want you to consult books during your research, so follow these steps:

1. Enter a keyword, such as nutrition, that will generate a reasonably sized list.
2. Examine the various entries in detail, starting with the most recent, to find books related to your topic.
3. In the stacks find and examine each book for relevance. *Tip:* While in the stacks examine nearby books, for they will likely treat the same subject.

CD-ROM, DVD, VHS

Encarta, Electronic Classical Library, Compton's Interactive Encyclopedia, and other reference disks are available. Browsing one of these sources can give you a good feel for the depth and strength of the subject and suggest a list of narrowed topics. Check with a librarian, a department office, and your instructor for discs and videos in a specialty area, such as mythology, poetry, or American history. These media forms can sometimes be found in local bookstores or by purchase over the Internet.

Using Textbooks and Reference Books

Dipping into your own textbooks can reward you with topic ideas, and a trip to the library to examine books and indexes in the reference room also can be beneficial.

Library Books and Textbooks

With your working topic in hand, do some exploratory reading. Carefully examine the **titles** of books, noting key terminology. Search a book's **table of contents** for topics. A history book on the American Civil War might display these headings:

> The Clash of Amateur Armies
> Real Warfare Begins
> The Navies
> Confederate High-Water Mark

If any heading looks interesting to you, go to the book's **index** for additional headings, such as this sample:

> Davis, Jefferson, President of the Confederate States
> evacuates Richmond, 574, 576
> foreign relations, 250, 251
> imprisonment of, 567
> inauguration, 52–53
> peace proposals, 564–65

Perhaps the topic on peace proposals will spur an interest in all peace proposals; that is, how do nations end their wars and send the troops home safely.

Reference Books

If you do not have access to an electronic database, refer to printed indexes, such as the *Readers' Guide to Periodical Literature, Bibliographic Index,* and *Humanities Index.* Searching in reference books under a keyword or phrase usually leads to a list of critical articles on the subject.

1b Writing a Thesis, an Enthymeme, or a Hypothesis

One central statement will usually control an essay's direction and content, so as early as possible, begin thinking in terms of a controlling idea. Each type shown below has a separate mission:

- A **thesis** advances a conclusion that the writer will defend: *Contrary to what some philosophers have advanced, human beings have always participated in wars.*

- An **enthymeme** uses a *because* clause to make a claim the writer will defend: *There has never been a "noble savage," as such, because even prehistoric human beings fought frequent wars for numerous reasons.*

- A **hypothesis** is a theory that must be tested in the laboratory, in the literature, and/or by field research to prove its validity: *Human beings are motivated by biological instincts toward the physical overthrow of perceived enemies.*

Let us look at each type in more detail.

Thesis Statement

A thesis expands your topic into a scholarly proposal, one that you will try to prove and defend in your paper. It does not state the obvious, such as: "Langston Hughes was a great poet from Harlem." That sentence cannot provoke an academic discussion because readers know that any published poet has talent. The writer must narrow and isolate one issue by finding a critical focus, such as this one:

> Langston Hughes used a controversial vernacular language that paved the way for later artists, even today's rap musicians.

This statement advances an idea that the writer can develop fully and defend with evidence. The writer has made a connection between the subject, *Langston Hughes,* and the focusing agent, *vernacular language.* A general thesis might state:

> Certain nutritional foods can prevent disease.

But note how your interest in an academic area can color the thesis:

HEALTH:	Nutritional foods may be a promising addition to the diet of those wishing to avoid certain diseases.
ECONOMICS:	Nutritional foods can become an economic weapon in the battle against rising health-care costs.
HISTORY:	Other civilizations, including primitive tribes, have known about food's nutritional values for centuries. We can learn from their knowledge.

A thesis sets in motion the writer's examination of specific ideas the study will explore and defend. Thus, when confronted by a general topic, such as "television," adjust it to an academic interest, as with "Video replays have improved football officiating but slowed the game" or "Video technology has enhanced arthroscopic surgery."

Your thesis is not your conclusion or your answer to a problem. Rather, the thesis anticipates your conclusion by setting in motion the examination of facts and pointing the reader toward the special idea of your paper, which you will save for the conclusion.

Enthymeme

Your instructor might want the research paper to develop an argument as expressed as an enthymeme, which is a claim supported with a *because* clause. Enthymeme has a structure that depends on one or more unstated assumptions.

> Hyperactive children need medication because ADHD is a medical disorder, not a behavioral problem.

The claim that children need medication is supported by the stated reason that the condition is a medical problem, not one of behavior. This writer will need to address the unstated assumption that medication alone will solve the problem.

Participating in one of the martial arts, such as Tae Kwan Do, is good for children because it promotes self-discipline.

The claim that one organized sporting activity is good for children rests on the value of self-discipline. Unstated is the assumption that one sport, the martial arts, is good for children in other areas of development, such as physical conditioning. The writer might also address other issues, such as aggression or a combat mentality.

Hypothesis

The hypothesis is a theory that needs testing to prove its validity, as well as an assumption advanced for the purpose of argument or investigation. Here is an example:

Discrimination against girls and young women in the classroom, known as "shortchanging," hinders the chances of women to develop their full academic potential.

This statement could produce a theoretical study if the student cites literature on the ways in which teachers "shortchange" students. A professional educator, on the other hand, would probably conduct extensive research in many classroom settings to defend the hypothesis with scientific observation.

Sometimes the hypothesis is *conditional:*

Our campus has a higher crime rate than other state colleges.

This assertion on a conditional state of being could be tested by statistical comparison.

At other times the hypothesis will be *relational:*

Class size affects the number of written assignments by writing instructors.

This type of hypothesis claims that as one variable changes, so does another, or that something is more or less than another. It could be tested by examining and correlating class size and assignments.

At other times, the researcher will produce a *causal* hypothesis:

A child's choice of a toy is determined by television commercials.

This causal hypothesis assumes the mutual occurrence of two factors and asserts that one factor is responsible for the other. The student who is a parent could conduct research to prove or disprove the supposition.

Thus, your paper, motivated by a hypothesis, might be a theoretical examination of the literature, but it might also be an actual visit to an Indian burial ground or a field test of one species of hybrid corn. Everything is subject to examination, even the number of times you blink while reading this text. See also pages 52–61 for more information on field research.

CHECKLIST: Narrowing a General Subject into a Working Topic

Unlike a general subject, a focused topic should:

☐ Examine one significant issue, not a broad subject.

☐ Argue from a thesis, enthymeme, or hypothesis.

☐ Address a knowledgeable reader and carry that reader to another plateau of knowledge.

☐ Have a serious purpose, one that demands analysis of the issues, argues from a position, and explains complex details.

☐ Meet the expectations of the instructor and conform to the course requirements.

1c Using Your Thesis to Chart the Direction of Your Research

Often, the thesis statement will set the direction of the paper's development.

Arrangement by Issues

The thesis statement might force the writer to address various issues and positions.

THESIS:	Misunderstandings about organ donation distort reality and set serious limits on the availability of those persons who need an eye, a liver, or a healthy heart.
Issue 1.	Many myths mislead people into believing that donation is unethical.
Issue 2.	Some fear that as a patient they might be put down early.
Issue 3.	Religious views sometimes get in the way of donation.

The outline above, though brief, provides three categories that require detailed research in support of the thesis. The note taking can be focused on these three issues.

Arrangement by Cause/Effect

In other cases, the thesis suggests development by cause/effect issues. Notice that the next writer's thesis on television's educational values points the way to four very different areas worthy of investigation.

THESIS:	Television can have positive effects on a child's language development.
CONSEQUENCE 1.	Television introduces new words.
CONSEQUENCE 2.	Television reinforces word usage and proper syntax.
CONSEQUENCE 3.	Literary classics come alive verbally on television.
CONSEQUENCE 4.	Television provides the subtle rhythms and musical effects of accomplished speakers.

The outline above can help the writer produce four positive consequences of television viewing.

Arrangement by Interpretation and Evaluation

Evaluation will evolve from thesis statements that judge a subject by a set of criteria, such as your analysis of a poem, movie, or museum display. Notice how the next student's thesis will require interpretation of Hamlet's character.

THESIS:	Shakespeare manipulates the stage settings for Hamlet's soliloquies to uncover his unstable nature and forecast his failure.
INTERPRETATION 1.	His soul is dark because of his mother's incest.
INTERPRETATION 2.	He appears impotent in comparison with the actor.
INTERPRETATION 3.	He is drawn by the magnetism of death.
INTERPRETATION 4.	He realizes he cannot perform cruel, unnatural acts.
INTERPRETATION 5.	He stands ashamed by his inactivity in comparison.

Arrangement by Comparison

Sometimes a thesis stipulates a comparison on the value of two sides of an issue, as shown in one student's preliminary outline:

THESIS:	Discipline often involves punishment, but child abuse adds another element: the gratification of the adult.
COMPARISON 1:	A spanking has the interest of the child at heart, but a beating or a caning has no redeeming value.
COMPARISON 2:	Time-outs remind the child that relationships are important and to be cherished, but lock-outs in a closet only promote hysteria and fear.
COMPARISON 3:	The parent's ego and selfish interests often take precedence over the welfare of the child or children.

CHECKLIST: Evaluating Your Overall Plan

1. What is my thesis? Will my notes and records defend and illustrate my proposition? Is the evidence convincing?
2. Have I found the best plan for developing the thesis with elements of argument, evaluation, cause/effect, or comparison?
3. Should I use a combination of elements; that is, do I need to evaluate the subject, examine the causes and consequences, and then set out the argument?

1d Drafting a Research Proposal

A research proposal helps to clarify and focus a research project. It comes in two forms: (1) a short paragraph to identify the project for approval of your instructor or (2) several pages to give background information, your rationale for conducting the study, a review of the literature, your methods, and the thesis, enthymeme, or hypothesis you plan to defend.

Writing a Short Research Proposal

A short proposal identifies five essential ingredients of your project:

1. The specific topic
2. The purpose of the paper (explain, analyze, argue)

3. The intended audience (general or specialized)
4. Your position as the writer (informer, interpreter, evaluator, reviewer)
5. The preliminary thesis or opening hypothesis

One writer developed this brief proposal:

> The world is running out of fresh water while we sip our Evian. However, the bottled water craze signals something—we don't trust our fresh tap water. We have an emerging crisis on our hands, and some authorities forecast world wars over water rights. The issue of water touches almost every facet of our lives, from religious rituals and food supply to disease and political instability. We might frame this hypothesis: Water will soon replace oil as the economic resource most treasured by nations of the world. However, that assertion would prove difficult to defend and may not be true at all. Rather, we need to look elsewhere, at human behavior, and at human responsibility for preserving the environment for our children. Accordingly, this paper will examine (1) the issues with regard to supply and demand, (2) the political power struggles that may emerge, and (3) the ethical implications for those who control the world's scattered supply of fresh water.

Writing a Detailed Research Proposal

A long proposal presents specific details concerning the project. It has more depth and a greater length than the short proposal, as shown above. The long proposal should include some or all of the following elements:

1. *Cover page* with title of the project, your name, and the person or agency to whom you are submitting the proposal (see pages 116–117 for details on writing titles and page 213 for the form of a title page).
2. An *abstract* that summarizes your project in 50 to 100 words.
3. A *purpose statement* with your *rationale* for the project (see the short proposal above for an example). Use explanation to review and itemize factual data. Use *analysis* to classify various parts of the subject and to investigate each one in depth. Use *persuasion* to question the general attitudes about a problem and then to affirm new theories, advance a solution, recommend a course of action, or—in the least—invite the reader into an intellectual dialogue.

4. A *statement of qualification* that explains your experience and perhaps the special qualities you bring to the project (i.e., you are the parent of a child with ADHD). If you have no experience with the subject, you can omit the statement of qualification.

5. A *review of the literature* that surveys the articles and books that you have examined in your preliminary work (see pages 101–109 for an explanation and an example of a review of literature).

1e Establishing a Schedule

The steps for producing a research paper have remained fundamental for many years. You will do well to follow them, even to the point of setting deadlines on the calendar for each step. In the spaces below, write dates to remind yourself when deadlines should be met.

____ *Finding and narrowing a topic.* Your topic must have a built-in question or argument so that you can interpret an issue and cite the opinions found in the source materials.

____ *Drafting a thesis and research proposal.* Even if you are not required to create a formal research proposal, you need to draft a plan to help direct and organize your research before you begin in-depth reading and research. See Section 1d.

____ *Creating notes.* Begin entering notes in a digital or printed research journal. Some notes will be summaries, while others might be exact quotations or paraphrases of the original material. Chapter 8 details the techniques for effective note taking.

____ *Organizing and outlining.* You may be required to create an organized, formal outline. Outlining and organizational models for your ideas are presented in Chapter 7.

____ *Drafting the paper.* During your writing, let your instructor scan the draft to give you feedback and guidance. The instructor may also encourage peer reviews, classroom workshops, and offer in-class review of your work in progress. See Chapter 9 for more details on drafting in an academic style.

____ *Formatting the paper.* Proper document design places your paper within the required format. Chapter 10 provides formatting for the research paper in MLA style.

____ *Writing a list of your references.* You will need to list the various sources used in your study. Chapter 10 provides documentation guidelines for MLA style.

___ *Revising and proofreading.* Be conscientious about examining your manuscript and making final corrections. Chapter 9 gives you tips on formatting, revision, and editing.

___ *Submitting the manuscript.* Like all writers, you will need at some point to "publish" your paper—on paper, on a disk, on a CD-ROM, or on your own Web site.

Gathering Sources in the Library

As the repository of the best books and periodicals, the library should be the center of your research, whether you access it electronically from your dorm room or visit it in person. The articles that you access through the library are, in the main, written by scholars and published in journals only after careful review by a board of like-minded scholars.

2a Launching the Library Search

In today's modern digital libraries, sources can be accessed just as easily as the Internet. In fact, many of the databases are part of the Web. Logged in at the library, you can download articles to your computer, print files, and read some books online. Your initial strategy will normally include three stages: the initial search to gauge the academic atmosphere for your subject, fine-tuning your focus for in-depth searching, and building your own electronic journal with a working bibliography, printouts, and downloaded items. In addition, it will benefit you to stroll through your library to identify its various sections and make mental notes of the types of information available there.

Begin your initial search at the library's electronic book catalog and electronic databases because they will:

- Show the availability of source materials representing diverse opinions.
- Provide a beginning set of reference citations, abstracts, full-text articles, and books, some with full text for printing or downloading.
- Help to restrict the subject and narrow your focus.
- Give an overview of the subject by showing how others have discussed it.

HINT

Today's college library not only houses academic books and periodicals, it connects you by the Internet to thousands of academic resources that you cannot reach any other way. So, when you visit your college library in person or by computer link, you can be assured of getting sources that have been reviewed carefully and judged worthy of your time and interest. There is no assurance of sources' legitimacy when you use a general Internet search engine, which cannot access the scholarship at the academic sites. A general search engine, such as Google or Lycos, might send you anywhere. The library's databases will send you to reputable sources.

2b Using the Library's Electronic Resources Catalog

Your library's computerized catalog probably has a special name, such as LIBNET, FELIX, ACORN, UTSEARCH, and so forth. It provides details on the various materials your library has available.

Books

The electronic book catalog lists every book in the library filed by subject, author, and title along with the call number, its location in the stacks, and its availability, as shown in this example:

> *Research: Successful Approaches* Elaine R. Monsen, ed.
> Subjects: Nutrition research / Dietetics research
> Location: General Book Collection, Level 3
> Call number: TX367.R46 2008
> Status: Available

In many cases, clicking on the title will give you an abstract of the book. In some cases the library's catalog will provide access to electronic books on the Internet, as shown by this example, which provides a URL hyperlink:

> *Nutrition in Early Life* [electronic resource]
> Edited by Jane B. Morgan and John W. T. Dickerson
> Internet access: http://www.library.tmc.edu

Journals

The electronic book catalog includes references to journals in bound volumes at the library or journals on the Internet, with links for accessing them.

> *Journal of Nutrition Education and Behavior*
> Availability: Periodicals Collection, Level 1
> This journal is available at the library.

> *The American Journal of Clinical Nutrition* [electronic resource]
> Internet access: Full text available from Highwire Press (Free Journals)
> http://highwire.stanford.edu/lists/freeart.dtl

This journal, not housed in the library, is found only by clicking on the hyperlink. We discuss this feature in the next section, 2c.

Internet Sites

The catalog includes links to Internet sites that the librarians have identified as excellent academic resources, such as this government document:

> *Food and Nutrition* [electronic resource]
> Washington, DC: Food and Nutrition Service, U. S. Dept. of Agriculture
> Internet access: Full text available from Health and Wellness Resource
> http://www.mhcc.edu/pages/1415.asp

Reference Books

The electronic catalog also lists reference books. It indexes by call number those housed in the library. Those available online have hypertext links.

> *Essay and General Literature Index*
> H. W. Wilson Company
> Location: Reference Stacks, Level 2
> Call number: A13.E752
> Status: Available

Social Sciences [electronic resource]
Internet access: Full text available from Columbia International
    Affairs Online
http://www.ciaonet.org/

Archives

Archival research takes you into past literature of a topic where you can
trace developing issues and ideas on a subject.

Archives of Dermatology [electronic resource]
Internet access: Full text available from the American Medical Association
http://archderm.ama-assn.org/

Bibliographies

Bibliographies list the works by a writer or the works about a subject.
They give you access to the titles of articles and books on your topic,
usually up to a certain date, as shown in the next example.

The Role of the Media in Promoting and Reducing Tobacco Use
National Cancer Institute, U. S. Dept of Health and Human Services
Internet access: http://dccps.nci.nih.gov/tcrb/monographs/19/
m19_complete.pdf

HINT

Many college libraries as well as public libraries are now part of a network of libraries. This network expands the holdings of every library
because one library will loan books to another. Therefore, if a book
you need is unavailable in your library, ask a librarian about an interli-
brary loan. Understand, however, that you may have to wait several
days for its delivery. Periodical articles usually come quickly by fax or
e-mail transfer.

2c Searching the Library's Electronic Databases

At the computer, search through the library's network of electronic
databases. You will find a list of these search engines at a link on the
library's home page, usually near the electronic book catalog. Each one
has a singular mission: to take you directly to articles on your subject,
with abstracts in most cases, and full text in many others. Thus, you can
print or download numerous documents, all relevant to your subject.

For example, InfoTrac is a popular database because it covers many subjects. This list gives a few of the sources found under the keyword *coffee*.

Drinking coffee slashes risk of Alzheimer's. Sylvia Booth Hubbard.
Newsmax (Jan 16, 2009) (287 words)
Full-Text

Shelf stable coffee. (New Products). Food Service Director. 22.1
(Jan 15, 2009): p. 48 (1). (70 words).
Full-Text

Java fuel. (biofuels BUZZ) (Brief article). Feedstuffs 81.1 (Jan 5,
2009): p. 19 (1). (189 words).
Full-Text

Clicking on an underlined hypertext accesses the article for your use. As shown above, the third source provides only a brief article, but the first two citations provide the full text of the article, which you can print or download to your files. Remember to save them as "text files."

General Databases

In addition to InfoTrac, there are many other general databases to serve your initial investigation. These databases are sometimes general in order to index many articles on a wide variety of topics. Start with one of these if you have a general keyword for your research but not a specific and focused topic.

BOOKS IN PRINT:
This database lists all books that are currently in print and available from publishers.

CQ RESEARCHER:
This collection provides in-depth reports on topics of current interest.

ENCYCLOPAEDIA BRITANNICA:
This reference covers all subjects with brief, well-organized articles.

FIRSTSEARCH:
This database covers a wide variety of topics and directs you to both articles and books.

GPO:
This site for the Government Printing Office gives you access to all government publications on all subjects.

INFORME!:
This database offers an index to articles in Spanish-language magazines.

INGENTA:	This site provides general information on a vast variety of topics. However, Ingenta is a commercial site, and you will have to pay for articles that you download or order by fax.
NETLIBRARY:	This database carries e-books on all subjects. To access a book online, you will need both a username and password, which are available from a librarian.
ONLINE BOOKS PAGE:	Maintained by the University of Pennsylvania, this site gives you access to books on all subjects with options for printing or downloading the pages.
OXFORD REFERENCE ONLINE:	This database offers you the full text of 135 reference books from Oxford University Press. The sources cover all general subjects. See your librarian to secure the username and password necessary for entry into the database.

By investigating two or three of the databases listed above, you should gain a quick start on your initial investigation into a subject. The sources that you download or print will help you focus your topic and frame your thesis.

Databases by Discipline

Your library also houses subject-specific databases. Thus, you can examine a specialized database for articles on health issues or, if you prefer, history, and many others. Listed next, by subject area, are a few databases to help launch your investigation. *Note:* These sources are only available through library access, and in some cases they require an additional username and password that you must request from your librarian.

Literature

CONTEMPORARY LITERARY CRITICISM:	This database indexes critical articles about contemporary authors, thus it is

LION:

a good source if you are examining the work of a twentieth-century writer.

This database contains full-text poems, drama, and fiction. It also includes biographies, literary criticism, guides to analysis of literary works, and video readings by writers.

LITFINDER:

This source helps you find poems, stories, plays, and essays.

MLA BIBLIOGRAPHY:

This major database provides access to all significant articles of criticism on literature, linguistics, and folklore.

History

AMERICA: HISTORY
AND LIFE:

This is a first-rate database of important articles on history.

WORLD HISTORY
FULLTEXT:

This is a database of full-text articles on all phases of world history.

VIVA:

This database focuses on history with an emphasis on women's studies.

Education, Psychology, and Social Issues

ERIC:

This giant database takes you quickly to articles and some books with a focus primarily on education but with full coverage of social and communication topics.

PROJECT MUSE:

This database contains current issues of about 200 journals in the fields of education, cultural studies, political science, gender studies, literature, and others. It also links you to JSTOR (see the next entry) for past issues of the journals.

JSTOR:

This acronym stands for "journal storage" because this database maintains the images of thousands of academic articles in their original form and with original page numbers. It centers on the social sciences but includes articles from other fields, such as literature.

PsycINFO: This database is a massive index to articles and books in psychology, medicine, education, and social work.

Health, Medicine, Fitness, and Nutrition

CINAHL: The initials stand for *Cumulative Index to Nursing & Allied Health Literature.* The giant database provides access to information in nursing, public health, and the allied fields of nutrition and fitness.

HEALTH AND WELLNESS: This database indexes a wide array of articles in medicine, nutrition, fitness, and public health.

PubMed: This source indexes articles on dentistry as well as nursing and medicine.

The Arts

GROVE DICTIONARY OF ART: This source is an online art encyclopedia, not a database. It contains information from the *Dictionary of Art* and features about 45,000 articles on painting, sculpture, architecture, and other visual arts.

GROVE DICTIONARY OF MUSIC: Like the one above, this source is an online encyclopedia. It has 29,000 articles drawn from the printed versions of *New Grove Dictionary of Music and Musicians, New Grove Dictionary of Opera,* and *New Grove Dictionary of Jazz.* It covers the various aspects of music, such as instrumentation, orchestral performance, voice, and so forth.

MUSIC INDEX: This database provides a citation index to 655 journals on a broad range of musical topics, including reviews. However, it is a citation-only database, so no abstracts or full-text are provided. On that note, however, see the Hint on page 27.

Computers, Business, Technology

GENERAL BUSINESS

FILE: This database provides abstracts and some full-text articles relating to issues in business and industry. It includes company profiles and some Wall Street reports.

SAFARI TECH BOOKS

ONLINE: This database focuses on e-commerce and computer science, with information on programming and technology management.

FAITS: Faulkner Advisory of IT Studies is a database of articles on wireless communications, data networking, security, the Internet, and product comparisons.

The Physical Sciences

AGRICOLA: This database provides an index to articles and book references in the areas of agriculture, animal, and plant sciences.

BIOONE: This site provides articles on the biological, ecological, and environmental sciences.

GEOREF: This database provides access to articles on geology and related subjects.

WILEY INTERSCIENCE: This database has articles on science and biochemistry.

The databases described above represent just a portion of those available at most college libraries, and more databases are being added monthly. Your task is to determine which databases are available at your library and react accordingly. Obviously, small libraries will not have the online resources that you will find at the library of a major university. If databases are limited, you may need to consult the printed bibliographies and indexes, as discussed in Section 2d.

HINT

If the databases to periodicals described above provide a citation but not the full text, you can probably retrieve the article in one of two ways: (1) try using the library's electronic book catalog (see 2b above) to retrieve the journal itself and thereby access the article, or (2) go into the stacks at your library, find the journal, and photocopy the article.

2d Searching the Printed Bibliographies

A bibliography tells you what books and articles are available for a specific subject. If you have a clearly defined topic, skip to page 28, "Searching the Specialized Bibliographies." If you are still trying to formulate a clear focus, begin with one of these general guides to titles of books to refine your search.

Searching in General Bibliographies

Some works are broad-based references to books on many subjects:

Bibliographic Index: A Cumulative Bibliography of Bibliographies (in print and online)
Where to Find What: A Handbook to Reference Books

Figure 2.1 shows how *Bibliographic Index* sends you to bibliographic lists inside books. In this case, the bibliography is found on pages 130–131 of King-Shaver and Hunter's book.

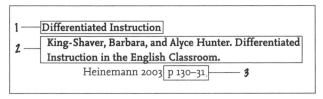

FIGURE 2.1
Example from *Bibliographic Index*, 2005, shows (1) subject heading, (2) entry of a book that contains a bibliography on the subject, (3) specific pages on which the bibliography is located.

If it fits your research, you would probably want to write a Works Cited entry for this source, as explained on pages 160–198. The MLA citation would look like this:

> King-Shaver, Barbara, and Alyce Hunter. *Differentiated Instruction in the English Classroom*. Portsmouth, NH: Heinemann, 2003. 130–131. Print.

Searching in the Specialized Bibliographies and Reference Works

After you have narrowed your subject, search one or two of the discipline-specific guides and bibliographies listed below. In the main, these are well-indexed references that will take you to more specific books. One of them can help you launch your investigation. Librarians at the reference desk can help you find them, and many are available online.

Humanities

Art	*Bibliographic Guide to Art and Architecture*
	Fine Arts: A Bibliographic Guide
Drama	*American Drama Criticism: Interpretations*
	Cambridge Guide to Theatre
History	*Dictionary of American History*
	Goldentree Bibliographies in History
Literature	*Dictionary of Literary Biography*
	Essay and General Literature Index
Music	*Music Reference and Research Materials*
	Bibliographic Guide to Music
Philosophy	*Oxford Companion to Philosophy*
	Research Guide to Philosophy
Religion	*Reference Works for Theological Research*
	Who's Who in Religion

Social Sciences

Business	*Bibliographic Guide to Business and Economics*
	Encyclopedia of Business Information Sources
Education	*Education: A Guide to Reference and Information Sources*

Social Sciences (continued)

Political Science	*International Bibliography of Political Science*
	Political Science: A Bibliographical Guide to the Literature
Psychology	*Annual Review of Psychology*
	Psychology: A Guide to Reference and Information Sources
	Bibliographical Guide to Psychology
Sociology	*Social Workers' Desk Reference*
	Sociology: A Guide to Reference and Information Sources
Speech	*Research and Source Guide for Students in Speech Pathology and Audiology*
Women's Studies	*American Women Writers: A Critical Reference Guide*
	Women's Studies Index

Sciences

Astronomy	*The Cambridge Atlas of Astronomy*
	Dictionary of Astronomy
Biology	*Henderson's Dictionary of Biological Terms*
	Information Sources in the Life Sciences
Chemistry	*How to Find Chemical Information: A Guide for Practicing Chemists, Teachers, and Students*
	Lange's Handbook of Chemistry
Computer Science	*Bibliographic Guide to the History of Computing, Computers, and the Information Processing Industry*
	Computer Science and Computing: A Guide to the Literature
Health	*Black's Medical Dictionary*
	Taber's Cyclopedic Medical Dictionary
Physics	*Information Sources in Physics*
	Physics Abstracts

2e   Searching the Printed Indexes

An index furnishes the exact page number(s) to articles in magazines, journals, and newspapers. When you have a well-developed idea of your topic, go to the specialized indexes of your discipline, such as *Music Index* or *Philosopher's Index* (either online at your library's computer or in print at the reference section of your library). If labeled an *index,* it may or may not include an abstract. If labeled as an index to *abstracts,* each entry will be an abstract. *Note:* An abstract is a brief description of an article, usually written by the author. An index to abstracts can accelerate your work by allowing you to read the abstract before you assume the task of locating and reading the entire work.

Starting with a General Index to Periodicals

A number of indexes are broad based and list articles in journals from many disciplines. These are good places to begin your research because the indexes have multiple entries and, in some cases, the articles are not as technical and scholarly as those indexed in specialized indexes. For general information on current events, consult *Readers' Guide to Periodical Literature,* which indexes such magazines such as *Aging, Foreign Affairs, Psychology Today, American Scholar, Scientific Review,* and many others. An entry from *Readers' Guide to Periodical Literature* follows:

> ANTIDEPRESSANTS
> The antidepressant tale: Figures signifying nothing?
> David Healey. Advances in Psychiatric Treatment v.12 p320–327 Sep 2006

Figure 2.2
From *Readers' Guide to Periodical Literature* showing subject, title, author, and publication data.

Make a Works Cited entry for your research journal if it looks promising:

Healey, David. "The Antidepressant Tale: Figures Signifying Nothing?"
    Advances in Psychiatric Treatment 12 (2006): 320–27. Print.

Searching Indexes to Topics in the Humanities

Humanities Index (in print or online) catalogs 260 publications in several fields:

archaeology	folklore	performing arts
classical studies	history	philosophy
language and literature	literary criticism	religion
area studies	political criticism	theology

MLA International Bibliography (in print or online) indexes most of the journals in language and literature studies. The printed versions are not kept up to date, so supplement the printed version with the electronic database, if available.

Abstracts of English Studies (in print or online) provides an excellent place to begin research in literature studies.

Dissertation Abstracts International—A: Humanities and Social Sciences (in print or online) provides an index to the abstracts of all American dissertations. In the print version, look for issue No. 12, Part 11, of each volume, for it contains the cumulated subject and author indexes for Issues 1–12 of the volume's two sections.

Searching Indexes to Topics in the Social Sciences

Social Sciences Index (in print or online) indexes journal articles for 263 periodicals in these fields:

anthropology	geography	political science
economics	law and criminology	psychology
environmental science	medical science	sociology

Dissertation Abstracts International—A: Humanities and Social Sciences (see above).

Searching Indexes to Topics in the Physical Sciences

Applied Science and Technology Index (in print or online) indexes articles in chemistry, engineering, computer science, electronics, geology, mathematics, photography, physics, and other related fields.

Biological and Agricultural Index (in print or online) indexes articles in biology, zoology, botany, agriculture, and related fields.

Dissertation Abstracts International—B: Sciences and Engineering (in print or online) provides an index to the abstracts of all American dissertations in the various fields of science and engineering. In the print version, look for issue No. 12, Part 11, of each volume, for it contains the cumulated subject and author indexes for Issues 1–12 of the volume's two sections.

Searching Indexes to Discipline-Specific Information

In addition to general indexes, you should examine indexes for your specific discipline. Numerous subject indexes are listed below in alphabetical order. Some will be available online through library access; others will be found in printed versions in the library's reference room.

Art Index	Mathematical Reviews
Biological Abstracts	Music Index
Business Periodicals	Nursing and Allied Health
Index	Literature, Cumulative
Chemical Abstracts	Index
Communication	Philosopher's Index
Abstracts	Physical Education Index
Computer Literature	Physics Abstracts
Index	Political Science
Economic Articles,	Abstracts,
Index of Education	International
Engineering Index	Psychological Abstracts
Environment Abstracts	Religion Index One
Geo Abstracts	Sociological Abstracts
Historical Abstracts	Women's Studies Index

2f Searching Biographies

Biographies of important people appear in books and articles, so you need to use a variety of sources. The electronic resources catalog (see 2b) is a place to start, using keywords such as "biography + index." It will access links to *Biography Index*, *Index to Literary Biography*, and many more. Alternatively, use the person's name as a keyword; for example, entering "Ben Franklin" will produce a reference to Cecil B. Currey's biography entitled *Ben Franklin: Patriot or Spy*.

In the library, examine these printed reference books:

Biography Index is a starting point for studies of famous persons. It will lead you to biographical information for people of all lands.

Current Biography Yearbook provides biographical sketches of important people. Most articles are three to four pages in length and include references to other sources at the end. It is current, thorough, and has international scope.

Contemporary Authors provides a biographical guide to current writers in fiction, nonfiction, poetry, journalism, drama, motion pictures, television, and a few other fields. It describes most contemporary writers. Entries include biographical facts, details on writings, and an overview of the author's work. A bibliography of additional sources is included.

Dictionary of Literary Biography provides a profile of thousands of writers in over 100 volumes under such titles as *American Humorists, Victorian Novelists,* and *American Newspaper Journalists.* A comprehensive index helps you locate the article on an author.

HINT

To find biographical reference works within a specific discipline, such as music or history, consult the library's electronic book catalog with a request such as "biographies of artists." It will then provide hyperlinks to Who's Who in American Art and other similar works.

2g   Searching Newspaper Indexes

Newspapers provide contemporary information. At the electronic catalog ask for a particular newspaper and then use its archival search engine to find articles on your topic. For example, asking for the Nashville *Tennessean* provides the link to the newspaper; by entering a search phrase, such as "state lottery," you gain access to articles in the current and previous editions of the *Tennessean,* as shown by this opening to an article:

Lawmaker: Home-schoolers shouldn't have tougher ACT mark
By DUREN CHEEK
Staff Writer
The **state's** top lawyer was asked yesterday whether Tennessee's **lottery**-funded scholarship program is unconstitutional because it requires home-schooled students to meet higher standards than others entering college.
The request for an opinion came from **state** Rep. Glen Casada, R-College Grove, who said he thinks requiring home-schooled students to score a 23 on their ACT to qualify, while public school students must score only 19, is unfair and discriminatory.
"Proponents of a **lottery** did not mention discriminating against home-schooled students in the **lottery** debate last fall," said Casada, referring to the **lottery** referendum last November. "Parents across the **state** were led to believe that students who met a certain criteria would receive a scholarship, period."

Figure 2.3
Opening paragraphs of an article in *The [Nashville] Tennessean.*

If your library's electronic catalog cannot access your specific newspaper, go to the Internet at **www.newspapers.com**. See pages 48–49 for more information.

In your library, visit also the contemporary reading room where you will find current issues of local and national newspapers on display for your reading pleasure or for research.

2h Searching the Indexes to Pamphlet Files

Librarians routinely clip items of interest from newspapers, bulletins, pamphlets, and miscellaneous materials and file them alphabetically by subject in loose-leaf folders. Make the pamphlet file a regular stop during preliminary investigation. Sometimes called the *vertical file*, it will have clippings on many topics, such as carpel tunnel syndrome, asbestos in the home, and medical care plans. Two helpful pamphlets, online and in print, are *SIRS* and *CQ Researcher*.

Social Issues Resources Series (SIRS) collects articles on special topics and reprints them as one unit on a special subject, such as abortion, AIDS, prayer in schools, pollution. With *SIRS* you will have ten or twelve articles readily available in one booklet.

The CQ Researcher, like *SIRS*, devotes one pamphlet to one topic, such as "Energy and the Environment." It will examine central issues on the topic, give background information, show a chronology of important events or processes, express an outlook, and provide an annotated bibliography.

HINT

For the correct citation forms to articles found in *SIRS* or *CQ Researcher*, see pages 188–191.

2i Searching Government Documents

All branches of the government publish and make available valuable material. The GPO database, maintained by the Government Printing

Office in Washington, DC, references this material. Your library may have this database, or you can access it on the Internet by entering **www.GPOAccess.gov** in your Web browser (see "Government," pages 42–43 for additional information). Just enter keywords in the search field to retrieve links to available documents. Your library might also house printed copies of these valuable reference tools:

Monthly Catalog of United States Government Publications indexes all the documents published by the Government Printing Office.

Public Affairs Information Service Bulletin (PAIS) indexes articles and documents published by miscellaneous organizations. Its excellent index makes it a good starting point.

Congressional Record provides Senate and House bills, documents, and committee reports.

Public Papers of the Presidents of the United States is the publication of the Executive Branch, including not only the president's papers but also the documents of all members of the president's cabinet and various agencies.

U.S. Code is the publication of U.S. Supreme Court decisions, codes, and other rulings.

HINT

See pages 181–182 for instructions on how to write a Works Cited entry for government documents.

2j   Searching for Essays Within Books

The *Essay and General Literature Index* (online and in print) helps you find essays hidden within anthologies. It indexes material of both a biographical and a critical nature. The essay listed in the example below might easily have been overlooked by any researcher.

King, Martin Luther, 1929–1968
    Raboteau, A. J. Martin Luther King and the tradition of black religious protest. (In Religion and the life of the nation; ed. by R. A. Sherrill, p. 46–65).

The library's electronic book catalog will give you the call number to Sherrill's book.

2k Building Your Research Journal

By now, you should have a collection of printed documents, photocopies, and downloaded files. It is important that you keep everything in order with sources clearly marked because you will need to make citations in your text to the authors and page numbers, and you will need a Works Cited page that lists full information on each source. These may seem like obvious tasks to you, but reminders are helpful, and too many students have had to abandon perfectly good quotations because they could not find full data on the source for the Works Cited entry.

Build a computer folder. Create a folder on your hard drive to store all the information you download during your research. Carry with you a zip or flash drive when you conduct research at the labs and library. Each time you download an article, save it so you can copy it to your folder. As you gather more and more data and begin building an outline, you might create more than one research folder.

Name each file precisely. Be descriptive in naming your files so you can identify the content after a few days. A file named *Brown* offers no clue to its contents except that "Brown" is probably the name of the author of an article. Instead, describe the contents— for example, *BrownPesticidesandPets.*

Organize a print folder. You will need a notebook with sleeves to keep your written notes, printouts, and photocopies. This, too, should be organized along the lines of your outline.

Build a rough outline. Early on, write a rough outline to help you organize the mass of material you are gathering. It will also help identify topics needing more research. See pages 88–90 for additional details.

Build a Works Cited file. As you discover sources that fit your outline or sources that you have slotted into your rough draft, enter them in your Works Cited file in alphabetical order. Thus, you will accomplish a major task as you work your way through the project. This working bibliography should, at a minimum, contain the author's name, the title of the work, publication information, and a library call number if it is a book you have not yet examined. Shown next is an example, in MLA style, of one student's Works Cited file in progress with three entries.

Works Cited

Phillips, Kate, and Esther D'Amico. "Chemical and Service Sector Demand to Rise." *Chemical Week* 17 Nov. 2008: 31–32. Print.

Ganoulis, Jacques G. *Risk Analysis of Pollution*. Hoboken, NJ: Wiley, 2009. Print.

Snyder, Shannyn. "Water Scarcity—The U.S. Connection." *The Water Project*. The Water Project, 2008. Web. 22 May 2008.

Gathering Sources Online

Electronic sources are a major source of research information, and we know that many students start their research with Internet sources. The Internet makes available millions of articles, illustrations, sound and video clips, and raw data relating to any subject. However, the Internet cannot replace the library references or field research. It offers the best and worst information, and requires careful evaluation. When reading an Internet article, always take time to judge its authority and veracity. This chapter will help you with two tasks: (1) to become an efficient searcher for academic information on the Web, and (2) to become accomplished at evaluating the complex web of Internet sites.

3a Beginning an Online Search

When you know your topic, perform a search using the words you would like to find in the title, description, or text of an Internet source. For example, to find information on California Governor Arnold Schwarzenegger's health care policies, you would enter the words *Arnold Schwarzenegger and health care*. The search engine will return a list of Web sites. You can then read through the list to find sites with articles relating to your research.

Using General Search Engines

About one hundred excellent search engines are available. Some of the more popular are listed below. Many sites entice you with advertisements for various products, but they do an excellent job of directing you to a wide variety of sources. Experiment with them and select the one that works best for you.

Subject directory search engines are compiled by humans and indexed to guide you to general areas that are then subdivided into specific categories. Your choice of a category controls the list.

About.com	**http://www.about.com**
Go.com	**http://go.com**
Yahoo	**http://www.yahoo.com**

Robot-driven search engines perform a keyword search by electronically scanning millions of Web pages. Your keyword phrase and Boolean operators control the list.

AltaVista	**http://www.altavista.com**
Excite	**http://www.excite.com**
Google	**http://www.google.com**

Find one you prefer, but keep in mind that search engines are designed in different ways. AltaVista, for example, will give you a massive number of results from its more than 22 million Web pages. Yahoo, on the other hand, is an edited site with directories and subdirectories.

Metasearch engines simultaneously query about ten major search engines, such as those listed above, and provide you with a short, relevant set of results. You get fewer results than would appear at one of the major search engines. For example, "chocolate + children" produced 342,718 hits on AltaVista, but only fifty on Mamma.com. A metasearch engine selects the first few listings from each of the search engines under this theory: each engine puts the most relevant results at the top of its list. This theory may or may not be true. Here are three metasearch engines:

Dogpile	**http://www.dogpile.com**
Mamma.com	**http://www.mamma.com**
Metacrawler.com	**http://www.metacrawler.com**

HINT

Most Web browser programs include a bookmark or favorites tool to allow you to save addresses of sites for quick access when revisiting the sites. Simply click on Bookmarks, then click on Add bookmark to automatically add the URL to the list of bookmarks. In Microsoft Internet Explorer, use the button bar marked Favorites to record an address. Bookmarks can easily be titled and organized so that you could have a Bookmark file devoted to a list of sites related to your research paper. *Note:* If you are working at a university computer laboratory, do not add bookmarks to the hard drive. Instead, save the bookmarks to your zip or flash drive by using Save As in the File menu.

3b Using Search Engines Devoted to Academic Disciplines

Many search engines specialize in one area, such as Edweb (education studies) or Envirolink (environmental studies). The following list contains sites that may be helpful in launching your investigation of Internet resources.

Humanities

Art

Art Resource **http://www.artres.com/c/htm/Home.aspx** This site features the world's largest stock photo archive with a keyword-searchable index.

World Wide Arts Resources **http://wwar.world-arts-resources.com** This site provides an artist index as well as an index to exhibits, festivals, meetings, and performances. Its search engine will take you to fine arts departments, online courses, syllabi, and art institutions.

History

Archiving Early America **http://www.earlyamerica.com** This site provides images of 18th-century documents for reading and downloading, such as the Bill of Rights and the speeches of Washington, Paine, Jefferson, and others.

The History Net **http://www.historynet.com** This site provides resources in the humanities and social sciences with links to wars and conflicts, air and sea battles, cultural studies, discovery and exploration.

Literature

EServer **http://eserver.org** This site provides academic resources in the humanities, including drama, fiction, film, television, and history.

Open Directory Project **http://www.dmoz.org/Arts/Literature** This site provides a directory, with links, to specific pieces of literature.

Voice of the Shuttle **http://vos.ucsb.edu** This site provides access to a massive collection of literary bibliographies, textual criticism, newsgroups, and links to classical studies, history, philosophy, and other related disciplines.

Philosophy

American Philosophical Association Internet site **http://www.apaonline.org** This site provides articles, bibliographies, software, a bulletin board, gopher server, and links to other philosophical sites containing college courses, journals, texts, and newsletters.

Episteme Links: Philosophy Resources on the Internet **http://www.epistemelinks.com** This site offers links to issues, traditions, biographies, philosophical movements, and full-text works.

> **HINT**
>
> If you have problems accessing a particular site, try truncating the address by cutting items from the end. For example, cut **http://www.emory.edu/WHSC/medweb.medlibs.html** to **http://www.emory.edu**. At this main page of the Web site, you can go in search of whatever site-related information you need.

Religion

Interfaith Online **http://www.interfaith.org** This comprehensive site gives references and resources on all religions and religious studies and religious organizations.

Vanderbilt Divinity School **http://www.divinity.library.vanderbilt.edu** A valuable source of references to and interpretations of the Bible, this site links to other religious Web sites and online journals, such as *Biblical Archaeologist*.

Social Sciences

Business

All Business Network **http://www.all-biz.com** This site provides current business articles with relevant information for the following—newsletters, organizations, news groups, and magazines.

Global Edge **http://globaledge.msu.edu/ResourceDesk** This site provides access to hundreds of articles and resource materials on banks, insurers, market news, jobs, and miscellaneous data.

Communication

Communication Resources on the Web **http://communication.utsa .edu/comsite/comresources.html** This site provides access to resources and Web sites on associations, book reviews, bibliographies, libraries, media, information science programs, and departments of communication in various universities.

Education

Educause **http://www.educause.com** This site focuses on educational and information technology. It has full-text articles from *Educause Review* and *Educause Quarterly*.

Edweb **http://www.edwebproject.org/resource.cntnts.html** This site focuses on educational issues and resource materials for grades K–12, with articles on Web education, Web history, and Web resources.

ERIC (Educational Resource and Information Center) **http://www .eric.ed.gov** ERIC is considered the primary source of research information for most educators. It contains about 1 million documents, available by a keyword search, on all aspects of teaching and learning, administration, and almost any topic related to the classroom. It includes lesson plans and bibliographies.

Government

Fedworld **http://www.fedworld.gov** This site links to Web sites of federal government departments as well as lists of helpful articles. It links to the Internal Revenue Service and other government agencies.

Library of Congress **http://www.loc.gov/index.html** This site provides access to the Library of Congress catalog online for books by author, subject, and title. It also links to historical collections and research tools, such as "Thomas," which provides access to congressional legislation.

White House Web **http://www.whitehouse.gov** This site provides a graphical tour, messages from the president and the vice president, and accounts of life at the White House. Visitors to this site can even leave a message for the president in the guest book.

Political Science

Political Science Resources on the Web **http://www.lib.umich.edu/govdocs/poliscinew.html** This site at the University of Michigan is a vast data file on government information—local, state, federal, foreign, and international. It is a good site for political theory and international relations information, with links to dissertations, periodicals, reference sources, university courses, and other social science information.

Psychology

Encyclopedia of Psychology **http://www.psychology.org/links/Resources/Doing_Research** This site features a collection of articles for preparing psychology documents from research. It has current and archival information.

PsycINFO **http://www.apa.org/psycinfo** The American Psychological Association maintains this excellent site of current and archival information in the various behavioral disciplines.

Sociology

Intute: Social Sciences **http://www.intute.ac.uk/socialsciences/lost.html** This site provides keyword access to Web sites in the social sciences.

Sociology **http://hakatai.mcli.dist.maricopa.edu/smc/ml/sociology.html** This site gives access to hundreds of sites that provide articles and resource materials on almost all aspects of sociology issues.

Women's Studies

Women's Resource Project **http://www.ibiblio.org/cheryb/women** This site links to libraries on the Web that have collections on Women's Studies. It also has links to women's programs and women's resources on the Web.

Women's Studies Database **http://www.mith2.umd.edu/Womens Studies/OtherWebSites/alpha.html** This site features a search engine for keyword searching women's issues and links to bibliographies, classic texts, references, course syllabi from various universities, and gateways to several other Web sites.

Sciences

Astronomy

American Astronomical Society **http://aas.org** This site has the full text of the *Astrophysical Journal,* providing articles, reviews, and educational information. The site also provides links to other astronomical sites on the Web.

Science at NASA **http://science.nasa.gov/Astronomy.htm** This site links to NASA programs, such as the space station, the shuttle program, and Project Galileo. It provides maps of the planets, views of Earth from many different angles, and plenty of planetary information.

Computer and Internet Technology

Computer Science **http://library.albany.edu/subject/csci.htm** This site provides numerous links to resources in the discipline.

Internet Society **http://www.isoc.org** This site is supported by the companies, agencies, and foundations that launched the Internet and that keep it functioning. It gives vital information published in the *ISOC Forum* newsletter.

Information Technology Services **http://www.utexas.edu/its/services/network** This site gives access to Internet and networking centers and relevant books, articles, and bibliographies.

Environmental Science

Envirolink **http://envirolink.org** This site has a search engine that provides access to environmental articles, photographs, action alerts, organizations, and additional Web sources.

Virtual Library of Natural Sciences and Mathematics **http://vlib.org/Science** This site provides valuable links to other Web sites in categories such as endangered species, global sustainability, and pollution.

General Science

Academy of Natural Sciences **http://www.ansp.org/library/index.php** This site has links to hundreds of articles and resource materials on various issues and topics in the natural sciences.

National Academies **http://www.nas.edu** This comprehensive site combines the resources of the National Academy of Sciences and Engineering, the Institute of Medicine, and the National Research Council. It focuses on math and science education, and it has links to scientific societies.

Thomson Reuters Scientific **http://scientific.thomsonreuters.org** This site provides searchable databases in biology and life sciences and serves as an excellent resource for students wishing to conduct scientific research.

Health and Medicine

Global Health **http://www.globalhealth.gov** This site provides articles on environmental destruction, overpopulation, infectious diseases, the consequences of war, and, in general, the health of the globe. It offers links to journals, newsletters, and government documents that explore environmental issues.

MedWeb: Medical Libraries **http://www.medweb.emory.edu/MedWeb** This site at Emory University connects with medical libraries and their storehouses of information. It also gives links to other health-related Web sites.

National Institutes of Health **http://www.nih.gov** NIH leads the nation in medical research, so this site provides substantive information on numerous topics, from cancer and diabetes to malpractice and medical ethics. It provides links to online journals for the most recent news in medical science.

HINT

You can quickly build a bibliography using the Internet in two ways: (1) at a search engine such as Google, enter a descriptive phrase, such as "child abuse bibliographies," and (2) at **www.amazon.com** and **www.barnesandnoble.com**, gather a list of books currently in print. Then, go in search of the books at your library.

3c Accessing Online Sources

Several types of online sources are available, and you should use more than one type in your research.

Internet Home Pages

You can locate home pages for individuals, institutions, and organizations by using a search engine, such as Yahoo or Google (see page 39). Just type in a person's name or the name of an organization in the search field. For example, a search for the American poet James Dickey will get a link to the site **http://www.jamesdickey.org**. A home page will provide links, a directory, an index, and an internal search engine that will take you quickly to specific material.

Internet Articles on the Web

A search engine will direct you to many articles on the Web, some isolated without documentation and credentials and others that list the author as well as the association to which the author belongs. For example, a search for "child care centers" will produce local sites, such as "Apple Tree Family Child Care." Private sites like these will infuse local knowledge to your research. Adding another relevant term, such as "child care regulations," will take you to state and national sites, such as the National Resource Center for Health and Safety in Child Care.

> **HINT**
>
> An Internet article that contains only a title and the URL cannot be properly documented and should be avoided.

Journal Articles on the Web

The Internet supplies journal articles of two types: (1) articles in online journals designed and published only on the Web, and (2) reproductions of articles that have appeared in printed journals. Find them in three ways.

- Using your favorite search engine, enter the keyword phrase *journals* plus the name of your subject. For example, one student using Google entered a keyword search for "journals + fitness" and found links to 20 journals devoted to fitness, such as *Health Page, Excite Health,* and *Physical Education.*

- Access a search engine's subject directory. In Yahoo, for example, one student selected "Social Science" from the key directory, clicked on Sociology, clicked on Journals, and accessed links to several online journals, such as *Sociological Research Online* and *Edge: The E-Journal of Intercultural Relations*.
- If you already know the name of a journal, go to your favorite search engine to make a title query, such as *Psycholoquy*.

Note: Some journals will furnish an abstract but then require a fee for access to the full text. The journals may also be available in library databases.

HINT

Remember that abstracts may not accurately represent the full article. In fact, some abstracts are not written by the author at all but by an editorial staff. Resist the desire to copy quotations from the abstract; instead, write a paraphrase or, better, find the full text and cite from it.

Magazine Articles on the Web

The Internet supplies magazine articles of two types. Some appear in original online magazines designed and published only on the Web. Others are reproductions of articles that have appeared in printed magazines. Several directories exist for finding magazine articles:

NewsDirectory.Com **http://www.newsdirectory.com** This site has directories of magazine home page links. Under "Current Events," for example, are *Atlantic Monthly* at theatlantic.com, *Harper's* at Harpers.org, and *Time* at time.com/time/. A magazine's archives can be searched at its site.

HighBeam Research **http://www.highbeam.com** This Web site has a subscription-based search engine to 17 million documents in newspapers, magazines, and news services. Free access is available for seven days; charges will accrue if membership is not canceled.

Pathfinder **http://pathfinder.com** This site gives free access to *Time Magazine* and thousands of archival articles.

ZD Net **http://www.zdnet.com** This site provides access to industry-oriented articles in banking, electronics, computers, and management. It offers two weeks of free access before charges begin to accrue.

You can also access online magazines through a search engine's directory. For example, using AltaVista, you can click on "Health and Fitness" in the subject directory of the home page, click next on "publications," then "magazines." The result is a list of 40 magazines devoted to various aspects of health and fitness, such as *Healthology* and *The Black Health Net*.

News Sources

Most major news organizations maintain Internet sites. Consult one of these:

CNN Interactive **http://www.cnn.com** This site features a good search engine that takes you quickly without cost to transcripts of CNN broadcasts. It is a good source for research in current events.

C-SPAN Online **http://www.c-span.org** This site emphasizes public affairs and offers both a directory and a search engine to transcripts. It is a valuable source for research in public affairs, government, and political science.

CQ Press Electronic Library **http://library.cqpress.com/index.php** This site keeps tabs on congressional activities in Washington.

National Public Radio Online **http://www.npr.org** This site provides audio articles downloaded using RealPlayer, Windows Media Player, or some other audio engine. Be prepared to take careful notes.

New York Times on the Web **http://www.nytimes.com** This site provides free access to recent articles. However, there is a fee for articles found in the 365-day archive. After purchase, articles appear on the monitor for printing or downloading.

USA Today DeskTopNews **http://www.usatoday.com** This site has a fast search engine and provides information about current events.

U.S. News Online **http://www.usnews.com** This site has a fast search engine and provides free, in-depth articles on current political and social issues.

Washington Times **http://www.washtimes.com** This site has up-to-the-minute political news.

To find additional newspapers, search for "newspapers" on Yahoo or Google. Your college library may also provide LEXIS-NEXIS, which will search online news sources for you.

Books on the Web

One of the best sources of full-text, online books is the Online Books Page at the University of Pennsylvania: **http://digital.library.upenn.edu/books**. This site indexes books by author, title, and subject. Its search engine takes you quickly to the full text of Thomas Hardy's *A Pair of Blue Eyes* or Linnea Hendrickson's *Children's Literature: A Guide to the Criticism*. This site adds new textual material almost every day, so consult it first. Understand, however, that contemporary books, still under copyright protection, are not included. That is, you can freely download an Oscar Wilde novel, but not one by contemporary writer J. K. Rowling. Here are a few additional book sites:

Bartleby.com	**http://www.bartleby.com**
Internet Classics Archive	**http://classics.mit.edu**
Project Gutenberg	**http://promo.net/pg**
Bibliomania	**http://www.bibliomania.com**
Education Planet	**http://educationplanet.com**
American Literary Classics	**http://www.americanliterature.com**

There are many more; in a search engine, use a keyword request for "full-text books."

E-mail Discussion Groups

Discussion groups correspond by e-mail on a central topic. For example, your literature professor might ask everybody in the class to join an e-mail discussion group on Victorian literature. To participate, you must have an e-mail address and subscribe to the list. In an online class using Blackboard, for instance, special forums can be designated that request the response of all members in the class. Your participation may contribute to your final grade.

Real-time chatting is also available through immediate messages on the Internet or with members of chat groups. However, we discourage the use of chat commentary for your research. Even though Yahoo, Google, AOL, and other servers offer access to chat groups, you cannot quote people with fictional usernames and no credentials.

Archives

In addition to searching the archives via your library's electronic catalog (see pages 19–21), you can find documents on the Internet.

1. For archival research in government documents, go to Library of Congress **http://www.loc.gov/index.html**. This site allows you to search by word, phrase, name, title, series, and number. It provides special features, such as an American Memory home page, full-text legislative information, and exhibitions, such as the various drafts of Lincoln's Gettysburg Address.

2. Go to an edited search engine, such as Yahoo, to find results quickly. For example, requesting "Native American literature + archives" produced links to Native American Press Archives, Native American History Archive, Native Americans and the Environment, Indigenous Peoples' Literature, and Sayings of Chief Joseph.

3. Go to a metasearch engine such as dogpile.com and make a request. For example, a search for "Native American literature + archives" lists such sites as Reference Works and Research Material for Native American Studies **http://www.stanford.edu**. At the Stanford site, you can find links to archives of Native American Studies Encyclopedias and Handbooks, Native American Studies Bibliographies, Native American Studies Periodical Indexes, and Native American Biography Resources.

4. Use the directory and subdirectories of a search engine and let them take you deeper and deeper into the files. Remember, this tracing goes quickly. Here is an example to show how the directories can carry you rather quickly from a browser's main page to archives of ancient warfare: AltaVista: Society > History > By Time Period > Ancient > Warfare in the Ancient World > The Legend of the Trojan War.

CHECKLIST: Evaluating Internet Sources

☐ Generally, using "edu" and "org" sites is preferable to using "com" sites because these domains usually are developed by an educational institution, such as Ohio State University, or by a professional organization, such as the American Psychological Association. Be sure to check authorship, currency, and other credentials. The "gov" (government) and "mil" (military) sites also usually have reliable materials.

☐ The "com" (commercial) sites become suspect for several reasons: (1) they are selling advertising space, (2) they often charge you for access to their files, and (3) they can be ISP (Internet service provider) sites where people pay to post material that has not been edited and subjected to peer review.

☐ What is the date? References in the sciences demand a date because research becomes out of date quickly. In like manner, look for the date when the Web information was last revised.

☐ Look for the professional affiliation of the writer, which you will find in the opening credits, or an e-mail address. Ask this question: Is the writer affiliated with a professional organization? Information should be included in the opening credit. An e-mail address might also show academic affiliation. Is contact information for the author or sponsoring organization included in the document? Other ways to investigate the credibility of a writer are searching for the writer's home page and by looking on Amazon.com for a list of his or her books.

☐ Can you identify the target audience? What does that tell you about the purpose of the Web site? Remember, the Web sites needed for your research should appeal to the intellectual person.

☐ What bias colors the Web site? *Note:* There will be a bias of some sort because even academic sites show bias toward, for example, the grandeur of Greek philosophy, the brilliance of the Allied Forces in World War II, or the artistry of Picasso's blue period.

☐ Look at the end of Internet articles for a bibliography of sources that indicate the scholarly nature of this writer's work.

☐ Treat e-mail as mail correspondence when using it as a scholarly source. Be sure the writer has solid credentials. Additionally, academic discussion groups may sometimes contain valuable information, but use it only if you know the source of the discourse.

☐ Do not cite from chat forums where fictitious usernames are common.

☐ Hypertext links to educational sites serve as an academic bibliography to reliable sources. However, if the site gives you hypertext links to commercial sites or if pop-up advertisements flood the screen, abandon the site and do not quote from it.

☐ Learn to distinguish among the different types of Web sites, such as advocacy pages, personal home pages, informational pages, and business and marketing pages. One site provides several evaluation techniques that might prove helpful: **http://its.unc.edu/t1/guides/irg-49.php**.

☐ Your skills in critical reading and thinking can usually determine the validity of a site. For more information on critical reading, visit this site: **http://www.virtualsalt.com**.

Conducting Field Research

Field research refers, in general, to studies conducted by researchers outside of the library. Computer technicians, microsurgeons, nuclear engineers, and other types of scientists and humanists conduct field research. Each discipline has different expectations in its methods of inquiry and presentation. The suggestions in this chapter will introduce you to the variety of field research and the results you might expect.

4a Conducting Research Within a Discipline

Some disciplines, more than others, will require you to work in the laboratory or the field, not just the library. Attitudes and methods differ in the social, physical, and applied sciences, and those three differ in many ways from the attitudes and methods of humanists.

The Social Scientists

Social scientists work from the assumption that behavior can be observed, tested, and catalogued by observation and experimental testing. Professionals perform thousands of experiments every month. They research stress in the workplace, study the effects of birth order on the youngest child, and develop testing mechanisms, such as the SAT test. As a student in the social sciences, you will be asked to perform similar but less exhaustive studies, such as observing "the typing mannerisms of students composing on a computer." If your topic examines any aspect of human behavior (for example, "road rage on campus streets"), prepare to go into the field for some aspects of your research.

The Physical Scientists

Physical scientists wish to discover, define, and explain the natural world. They operate under the assumption that we can obtain precise data on flora and fauna, geological formations, the various species of animals, and so forth. You may be asked to join a field expedition to catalog one type of fern, to test the water conditions at a local lake, or to locate sinkholes in a confined area. Laboratory experimentation is also a regular feature for scientists. Any experiments that you conduct should be recorded in a lab notebook because they may become significant to your written reports. If your topic examines the natural world in some way—for example, "the growing deer population in Governor's Manor subdivision"—field research may be useful.

The Applied Scientists

Applied scientists *apply* the knowledge they acquire to make life more efficient, enduring, and comfortable. By mathematical formulas and cutting-edge technology, they launch spaceships to encircle the globe, find new ways to repair broken bones, and discover better methods of movie animation. You, too, can participate in such experiments by designing access facilities for students with wheelchairs (for example, should doors open out or open in?), investigating systems to measure the force of lightning strikes, or examining ways to increase the weight of beef cattle. It is not unusual today for undergraduate students to apply their computer knowledge to the creation of new programs, even new software and hardware. If your research involves application of scientific information, researching in the field may help you formulate your ideas.

The Humanists

Humanists in the fine arts, literature, history, religion, and philosophy have a distinctive approach to knowledge. While scientists usually investigate a small piece of data and its meaning, humanists examine an entire work of art (Verdi's opera *Rigoletto*), a period of history (the Great Depression), or a philosophical theory (existentialism). Humanists usually accept a poem or painting as a valid entity and search it subjectively for what it means to human experience. However, that fact does not preclude humanists from conducting field research. For example, a student might go to England to retrace the route of the pilgrims in their journey to Canterbury. Such a trip might shed new light on Chaucer's poetry. In another instance, a student's field trip to Jackson, Mississippi, might enlighten the scholar on the fiction of Eudora Welty. Conducting archival research on manuscript materials could take you into unknown territory. Your work with a writer living in your locality may prompt you toward a personal interview. And correspondence with writers and historians is standard fare in humanist research. Thus, if your research in history, religion, or the arts offers the opportunity for field research, add it to your research program.

4b   Investigating Local Sources

Interviewing Knowledgeable People

Talk to persons who have experience with your subject. Personal interviews can elicit valuable in-depth information. They provide information that few others will have. Look to organizations for experienced persons. For example, a student writing on a folklore topic might contact the county historian, a senior citizens organization, or a local historical society. If necessary, the student could post a notice soliciting help: "I am writing a study of local folklore. Wanted: people who have knowledge of regional tales." Another way to accomplish this task is to request information from an e-mail discussion group, which will bring responses from several persons (see page 49 for more details).

Follow a few general guidelines:

- Set up your appointments in advance.
- Consult with persons knowledgeable about your topic.
- If possible, talk to several people to get a fair assessment.
- A telephone interview is acceptable, as is e-mail correspondence.
- Be courteous and arrive on time for interviews.
- Be prepared in advance with a set of focused, relevant questions.
- For accuracy and if permitted by the person being interviewed, record the session with an audio or videotape.

- Double-check direct quotations with the interviewee or the tape.
- Get permission before citing a person by name or quoting the person's exact words.
- Handle private and public papers with great care, and send participants a copy of your report along with a thank you note.

When finished, make a works cited entry just as you would for a book:

Thornbright, Mattie Sue. "Growing Greens in Georgia." Personal interview. Jonesboro, Georgia. 15 Jan. 2010. MS.

Writing Letters and Corresponding by E-mail

Correspondence provides a written record for research. Write a letter that asks pointed questions that will elicit relevant responses. Tell the person who you are, what you are attempting to do, and why you are writing to him or her.

Odette Ogburu
1551 Grayside Road
Topeka, KS

Ms. Evelyn Casasola, Principal
Parkview Elementary School
Topeka, KS

Dear Ms. Casasola:

I am a college student conducting research into methods for handling hyperactive children in the public school setting. I am surveying each elementary school principal in Auburn-Washburn School District. I have contacted the central office also, but I wished to have perspectives from those of you on the frontlines. I have a child with ADHD, so I have a personal as well as a scholarly reason for this research. I could ask specific questions on policy, but I have gotten that from the central office. What I would like from you is a brief paragraph that describes your policy and procedure when one of your teachers reports a hyperactive child. In particular, do you endorse the use of medication for calming the child? May I quote you in my report; I will honor your request to withhold your name.

I have enclosed a self-addressed, stamped envelope for your convenience. You may e-mail me at oogburu@washburn.edu.

Sincerely,

Odette Ogburu

This letter makes a fairly specific request for a minimum amount of information. It does not require an expansive reply. Should Ogburu use a quotation from the reply, she would provide a bibliography entry on her Works Cited page.

> Casasola, Evelyn. Principal of Parkview Elementary School, Topeka, KS. Message
> to the author. 5 Apr. 2006. E-mail.

Note: If Ogburu decided to build a table or graph from the nine replies of the various principals, she would need to document the survey in a Works Cited entry as shown on page 59.

Reading Personal Papers

Search out letters, diaries, manuscripts, family histories, and other personal materials that might contribute to your study. The city library may house private collections, and the public librarian might help you contact the county historian and other private citizens who have important documents. Obviously, handling private papers must be done with the utmost decorum and care. Make a Works Cited entry for such materials.

> Joplin, Barry. "Notes on Robert Penn Warren." Unpublished paper. Nashville.
> 19 Oct. 2009. MS.

Attending Lectures and Public Addresses

Watch bulletin boards and the newspaper for a public speaker who may contribute to your research. At the lecture, take careful notes, and if the speaker makes one available, secure a copy of the lecture or speech. If you want to use your equipment to make an audio or videotape of a speech, courtesy demands that you seek permission. Remember that many lectures, reproduced on video, are available in the library or in departmental files. Always make a Works Cited entry for any words or ideas you use.

> Petty-Rathbone, Virginia. "Edgar Allan Poe and the Image of Ulalume."
> Lecture. Heard Library, Vanderbilt U., 25 Jan. 2010. Address.

Investigating Government Documents

Documents are available at four levels of government: city, county, state, and federal. As a constituent, you are entitled to examine a wide assortment of records on file at various agencies. If your topic demands it, you may contact the mayor's office, attend and take notes at a meeting of the county commissioners, or search for documents in the archives of the state or federal government.

City and County Government

Visit the courthouse or county clerk's office to find facts on elections, marriages, births, and deaths, as well as census data. Local archives house wills, tax rolls, military assignments, deeds to property, and much more. A trip to the local courthouse can help you trace the history of the land and its people.

State Government

Contact a state office that relates to your research, such as Consumer Affairs (general information), Public Service Commission (which regulates public utilities such as the telephone company), or the Department of Human Services (which administers social and welfare services). The names of these agencies may vary from state to state. Each state has an archival storehouse and makes its records available for public review.

Federal Government

The Government Printing Office provides booklets and publications. A list of these materials, many of which are free, appears on the Web site of the government printing office, www.GPOAccess.gov. In addition, you can visit the National Archives Building in Washington, DC, or one of the regional branches in Atlanta, Boston, Chicago, Denver, Fort Worth, Kansas City, Los Angeles, New York, Philadelphia, or Seattle. Their archives contain court records and government documents. Before going, review *Guide to the National Archives of the United States, Select List of Publications of the National Archives and Record Service,* and the *Catalog of National Archives Microfilm Publications.*

4c Examining Audiovisual Materials, the Internet, and Television

Important data can be found in audiovisual materials. You will find these both on and off campus. Consult such guides as *Educators Guide* (film, filmstrips, and tapes), *Media Review Digest* (nonprint materials),

Video Source Book (video catalog), *The Film File,* or *International Index to Recorded Poetry* to find relevant titles. Television, with its many channels, such as *The History Channel,* offers invaluable data in programs that you can record for later detailed examination. The Internet, as discussed earlier, provides multimedia on almost every conceivable topic. As with other sources, write Works Cited entries for any materials that have merit and contribute to your paper.

> Reed, Philip. "Car Loans." Interview. CNN. Cable News Network, 23 Feb. 2009. Television.

When using media sources, watch closely the opening and closing credits to capture the necessary data for your Works Cited entry. The format is explained on pages 160–168. As with the personal interview, be scrupulously accurate in taking notes. Citations may refer to a performer, director, or narrator, depending on the focus of your study. It is best to write direct quotations because paraphrases of television commentary can unintentionally be distorted by bias. Always scrutinize material taken from an Internet site (see pages 50–51 for a checklist of ways to evaluate Internet articles).

4d Conducting a Survey with a Questionnaire

Questionnaires can produce current, firsthand data that you can tabulate and analyze. To achieve meaningful results, you must survey randomly with regard to age, sex, race, education, income, residence, and other demographic factors. Bias can creep into the questionnaire unless you remain objective. Use a formal survey only if you are experienced with tests and measurements and statistical analysis or when you have an instructor who will help you with the instrument. Be advised that most schools have a Human Subjects Committee that sets guidelines, draws up consent forms, and requires anonymity of participants for information gathering that might be intrusive. An informal survey gathered in the hallways of campus buildings lacks credibility in the research paper. If you decide to build a table or graph from survey results, first review the example on page 221 in the appendix.

Surveys usually depend on *quantitative* methodologies, which produce numerical data. That is, the questionnaire results can be tallied to itemize such things as campus crime rates, parking slots for students, or the shift in student population to off-campus housing. In some cases, surveys depend on *qualitative* methodologies, which answer questions on social issues, such as the number of biased words in a history text, the reasons for marijuana use, or levels of hyperactivity in a test group of children.

Reference your project survey in the Works Cited section of your paper.

Castor, Diego, and Carmen Aramide. "Child Care Arrangements of
    Parents Who Attend College." Coeur d'Alene: North Idaho College,
    2008. Survey.

Keep the questionnaire short, clear, and focused on your topic. Questions must be unbiased. Ask your professor to review the instrument before using it. Design your questionnaire for a quick response to a scale ("Choose A, B, or C"), to a ranking (first choice, second choice, and so on), or to fill-in blanks. You should also arrange for an easy return of the questionnaire by providing a self-addressed stamped envelope or by allowing respondents to send in their completed questionnaires by e-mail.

Tabulate the responses objectively. Present the results—positive or negative—as well as a sample questionnaire in the appendix to your paper. While results that deny your hypothesis may not support the outcome you desire, they still have value.

4e   Conducting Experiments, Tests, and Observation

Empirical research, performed in a laboratory or in the field, can determine why and how things exist, function, or interact with one another. Your paper will explain your methods and findings in pursuit of a hypothesis or theory. An experiment thereby becomes primary evidence for your paper.

Observation occurs generally in the field, which might be at a childcare center, a movie theater, a parking lot, or the counter of a McDonald's restaurant. The field is anywhere you can observe, count, and record behavior, patterns, and systems. It can be testing the water in a stream or observing the nesting patterns of deer. Retail merchandisers conduct studies to observe buying habits. A basketball coach might gather and analyze shot selections by members of his team.

A *case study* is a formal report based upon your observation of a human subject. For it, you might have to examine patterns of behavior to build a profile. It can be based on biographical data, interviews, tests, and observation. For example, you might observe and interview an older person with dementia, and that would be a case study and evidence for your research paper. Each discipline has its own standards for properly conducting a case study. You should not examine any subject without the guidance and approval of your instructor.

Most experiments and observations begin with a *hypothesis*, which is similar to a thesis (see pages 9–12). The hypothesis is a statement assumed to be true for the purpose of investigation. *Hummingbirds live as extended families governed by a patriarch* is a hypothesis needing data to prove its validity. *The majority of people will not correct the poor grammar of a speaker* is a hypothesis that needs testing and observation to prove its validity.

You can begin observation without a hypothesis and let the results lead you to the implications. Shown below is one student's double-entry format used to record observation on the left and commentary on the right. It is a limited example of field notes.

Record:	Response:
Day 1	
10-minute session at window, three hummingbirds fighting over the feeder	Is the male chasing away the female or is the female the aggressor?
Day 2	
10-minute session at window, saw eight single humming birds at feeder #1 and one guarding feeder #2 by chasing others away	I did some research and the red-throated male is the one that's aggressive.

Generally, a report on an experiment or observation follows a format that provides four distinct parts: introduction, method, results, and discussion. These four divisions of the scientific report are discussed fully in Section 7a, page 79.

CHECKLIST: Conducting an Experiment or Observation
☐ Express clearly your hypothesis in the introduction.
☐ Provide a review of the literature if necessary for establishing an academic background for the work.

☐ Explain your design for the study-lab experiment, observation, or the collection of raw data in the field.

☐ Design the work for maximum respect to your subjects. In that regard, you may find it necessary to get approval for your research from a governing board.

☐ For the results section, maintain careful records and accurate data. Don't let your expectations influence the results.

☐ Be prepared in your conclusion to discuss your findings and any implications to be drawn.

Understanding and Avoiding Plagiarism

This chapter defines plagiarism, explores the ethical standards for writing in an academic environment, and provides examples of the worst and best of citations. Plus, we face the newest problem: the Internet making it easy to copy and download material and paste it into a paper—which in itself is not a problem *unless* you fail to acknowledge the source.

Intellectual property has value. If you write a song, you have a right to protect your interests. Thus, the purpose of this chapter is to explore with you the ethics of research writing, especially about these matters:

- Using sources to enhance your credibility
- Using sources to place a citation in its proper context
- Honoring property rights
- Avoiding plagiarism
- Honoring and crediting sources in online course work

5a Using Sources to Enhance Your Credibility

What some students fail to realize is that citing a source in their papers, even the short ones, signals something special and positive to readers—that the student has researched the topic, explored the literature about it, and has the expertise to share it. By announcing clearly the name of a source, the writer reveals the scope of his or her critical reading in the literature, as shown in these notes by one student:

> Americans consume an average of 300-plus liters of water per day per capita while the average person needs only 20 to 40 liters, according to O'Malley and Bowman.

> Sandra Postel says water is "a living system that drives the workings of a natural world we depend on" (19).

> Postel declares: "A new water era has begun" (24). She indicates that the great prairies of the world will dry up, including America's. Hey, when folks in America notice the drought, then maybe something will happen.

If transferred into the paper, these notes will enable readers to identify the sources used. The notes give clear evidence of the writer's investigation into the subject, and they enhance the student's image as a researcher. The student will get credit for displaying the sources properly. The opposite, plagiarism, presents the information as though it were the student's own:

> The great prairies of the world will soon dry up, and that includes America's, so a new water era has begun.

That sentence borrows too much. If in doubt, also cite the source and place it within its proper context. This issue will be further explained in Section 5d.

5b Identifying Bias in a Source

You will show integrity in your use of sources by identifying any bias expressed by a writer or implied by the political stance of a magazine. For example, if you are writing about federal aid to farmers, you will find different opinions in a farmer's magazine and a journal that promotes itself as a watchdog of federal spending. One is an advocate and the other a vocal opponent. You may quote them, but only if you identify them carefully. Let's examine the problem faced by one student. In researching articles on the world's water supply, Norman Berkowitz found an article of interest but positioned it with a description of the source, as shown in this note that carefully identifies the source of an alarmist attitude.

Earth First, which describes itself as a radical environmental journal, features articles by an editorial staff that uses pseudonyms, such as Sky, Jade, Wedge, and Sprig. In the article "The End of Lake Powell," Sprig says, "The Colorado River may soon be unable to provide for the 25 million people plumbed into its system" (25). The danger, however, is not limited to Lake Powell. Sprig adds, "This overconsumption of water, compounded with a regional drought cycle of 15 years, could mean that Lake Powell and every other reservoir in the upper Colorado River area will be without water" (24–25).

Be a responsible writer: Examine articles, especially those in magazines and on the Internet, for special interests, opinionated speculation, or an absence of credentials by the writer. Be wary of Web sites without an academic or government sponsor. Refer to Chapter 3, which lists the most reliable databases for evidence-based sources.

5c Honoring Property Rights

If you invent a new piece of equipment or a child's toy, you can get a patent that protects your invention. You now own it. If you own a company, you can register a symbol that serves as a trademark for the products produced. You own the trademark. In like manner, if you write a set of poems and publish them in a chap book, you own the poems. Others must seek your permission before they can reproduce the poems, just as others must not use your trademark or pay to produce your toy.

The principle behind the copyright law is relatively simple. Copyright begins at the time a creative work is recorded in some tangible form—a written document, a drawing, a tape recording. It does not depend upon a legal registration with the copyright office in Washington, DC, although published works are usually registered. The moment you express yourself creatively in any medium—on paper, on a canvas, electronically, and so on—that expression is your intellectual property. You have a vested interest in any profits made from the distribution of your work. For that reason, songwriters, cartoonists, fiction writers, and other artists guard their work and do not want it distributed without compensation.

In scholarly work there is seldom compensation, but there is certainly the need for recognition. We do that by providing in-text citations and bibliography entries. As a student you may use copyrighted material in your research paper under a doctrine of *fair use* as described in the U.S. Code, which says:

> The fair use of a copyrighted work . . . for purposes such as criticism, comment, news reporting, teaching (including multiple copies for classroom use), scholarship, or research is not an infringement of copyright.

Thus, as long as you borrow for educational purposes, such as a paper to be read by your instructor, you should not be concerned about violating the copyright law, as long as you provide documentation. However, if you decide to *publish* your research paper on a Web site, then new considerations come into play and you should seek the advice of your instructor.

5d Avoiding Plagiarism

Plagiarism is offering the words or ideas of another person as one's own. Major violations, which can bring failure in the course or expulsion from school, are:

- The use of another student's work
- The purchase and submission of a "canned" research paper
- Copying passages into your paper without documentation
- Copying a key, well-worded phrase without documentation
- Placing specific ideas of others into your own words without documentation
- Inadequate or missing citations
- Missing quotation marks
- Incomplete or missing Works Cited entries

Whether deliberate or not, these instances all constitute forms of plagiarism. Closely related but not technically plagiarism is fabrication of information—that is, making up material off the top of your head. Some newspaper reporters have lost their jobs because of such fabrication.

There are a number of steps you can take to avoid plagiarism. First, develop personal notes full of your own ideas on a topic. Discover what you think and how you feel about the issue. Then, rather than copying sources one after another, express your own ideas at the beginning of paragraphs and then synthesize the ideas of others by using summary, paraphrase, and quotation. Rethink and reconsider ideas gathered by your reading, make meaningful connections, and when you refer to a specific source—as you inevitably will—give it credit.

Unintended plagiarism can result from student carelessness. Failing to enclose quoted material within quotation marks even though an in-text citation is given or paraphrase that never quite becomes paraphrase because too much of the original is left intact are both examples of carelessness leading to plagiarism. In this area, instructors might step in and help the beginning researcher, for although these cases are not flagrant instances of plagiarism, these errors can mar an otherwise fine piece of research.

There is one safety net: Express clearly the name of your sources to let readers know the scope of your reading on the subject, as in this note:

> Commenting on the emotional role that music has on our lives, editor Marc Smirnoff makes this observation in *Oxford American:* "The music that human beings rely on is essential to them. We know which tunes to listen to when we need an all-important lift (or when the party does) or when we want to wallow in our sadness" (4).

Citations like the one above help establish your credibility because they make clear the sources that you have read and how your ideas blend with the source.

CHECKLIST: Documenting Your Sources

☐ Let readers know when you begin borrowing from a source by introducing a quotation or paraphrase with the name of the authority.

☐ Enclose within quotation marks all quoted materials—keywords, phrases, sentences, or paragraphs.

☐ Make certain that paraphrased material has been rewritten into your own style and language. The simple rearrangement of sentence patterns is unacceptable.

☐ Provide specific in-text documentation for each borrowed item, but keep in mind that styles differ for MLA, APA, CMS, and CSE standards. These styles are explained in later chapters.

☐ Provide a bibliographic entry in the Works Cited section for every source cited in the paper.

Common Knowledge Exceptions

Common knowledge exceptions exist because you and your reader will share the same perspectives on a subject. For example, if you attend the University of Delaware, you need not cite the fact that Wilmington is Delaware's largest city, or that Dover is the capital city.

Information of this sort requires *no* in-text citation because your local audience will be knowledgeable:

> The extended shoreline of Delaware provides one of the most extensive series of national wildlife refuges in the eastern United States. The state stretches from its northern border with Pennsylvania to form a 100-mile border with Maryland to its west and south. Its political center is Dover in the center of the state, but its commercial center is Wilmington, a great industrial city situated on Delaware Bay just below Philadelphia.

However, a writer in another place and time might need to cite the source of this information. Most writers would probably want to document this next passage.

> Early Indian tribes on the plains called themselves *Illiniwek* (which meant strong men), and French settlers pronounced the name *Illinois* (Angle 44).

Common factual information that one might find in an almanac, fact book, or dictionary need not be cited. Here is an example:

> President George H. W. Bush launched the Desert Storm attack in 1991 against Iraq and its leader Saddam Hussein with the support of allies and their troops from several nations. His son, President George W. Bush, launched a similar attack in 2003 against the same dictator and his army.

The passage needs no documentation, but the farther we move in history from that time and place, the more likely will be the need for documentation. Of course, provide a citation for analysis that goes beyond common facts.

CHECKLIST: Required Instances for Citing a Source

1. An original idea derived from a source, whether quoted or paraphrased. This next sentence requires an in-text citation and quotation marks around a key phrase.

   > Genetic engineering, by which a child's body shape and intellectual ability is predetermined, raises for one source "memories of Nazi attempts in eugenics" (Riddell 19).

2. Your summary of original ideas by a source.

   > Genetic engineering has been described as the rearrangement of the genetic structure in animals or in plants, which is a technique that takes a section of DNA and reattaches it to another section (Rosenthal 19–20).

3. Factual information that is not common knowledge within the context of the course.

> Genetic engineering has its risks: a nonpathogenic organism might be converted into a pathogenic one or an undesirable trait might develop as a result of a mistake (Madigan 51).

4. Any exact wording copied from a source.

> Kenneth Woodward asserts that genetic engineering is "a high stakes moral rumble that involves billions of dollars and affects the future" (68).

5e Sharing Credit in Collaborative Projects

Joint authorship is seldom a problem in collaborative writing, especially if each member of the project understands his or her role. Normally, all members of the team receive equal billing and credit. However, it might serve you well to predetermine certain issues with your peer group and the instructor:

- How will the project be judged and grades awarded?
- Will all members receive the same grade?
- Can a nonperformer be dismissed from the group?
- Should each member write a section of the work and everybody edit the whole?
- Should certain members write the draft and other members edit and load it onto a CD or onto the Web?
- Can the group work together via e-mail rather than meeting frequently for group sessions?

Resolving such issues at the beginning of a project can go a long way toward eliminating entanglements and disagreements later.

5f Seeking Permission to Publish Material on Your Web Site

You may wish to include your research papers on your personal Web site if you have one. However, the moment you do so, you are *publishing* the work and putting it into the public domain. That act carries responsibilities. In particular, the *fair use* doctrine of the U.S. Code refers to the personal educational purposes of your usage. When you load borrowed images, text, music, or artwork onto the Internet, you are making that intellectual property available to everybody all over the world.

Short quotations, a few graphics, and a small quantity of illustrations to support your argument are examples of fair use. Permission will be needed, however, if the amount you borrow is substantial. The borrowing cannot affect the market for the original work, and you cannot misrepresent it in any way. The courts are still refining the law. For example, would your use of three *Doonesbury* comic strips be substantial? Yes, if you reproduce them in full. Would it affect the market for the comic strip? Perhaps. Follow these guidelines:

- Seek permission for copyrighted material that you publish within your Web article. Most authors will grant permission at no charge. The problem is tracking down the copyright holder.
- If you make the attempt to get permission, and if your motive for using the material is *not for profit*, it is unlikely you will have any problem with the copyright owner. The owner would have to prove that your use of the image or text caused the owner financial harm.
- You may publish without permission works that are in the public domain, such as a section of Nathaniel Hawthorne's *The Scarlet Letter* or a speech by the president from the White House. In general, creative works enter the public domain after 75 years (the laws keep changing). Government papers are public domain.
- Document any and all sources that you feature on your Web site.
- If you provide hypertext links to other sites, you may need permission to do so.
- Be prepared for other persons to visit your Web site and even borrow from it. Decide beforehand how you will handle requests for use of your work, especially if it includes your creative efforts in poetry, art, music, or graphic design.

HINT

For information on the Fair Use Laws, visit http://fairuse.stanford.edu/Copyright_and_Fair_Use_Overview/index.html.

Reading and Evaluating Sources

Finding sources worthy of citation in your paper can be a challenge. This chapter cuts to the heart of the matter: How do you find the best, most appropriate sources? Should you read all or just part of a source? How do you respond to it? Also, in this age of electronic publications, you must continually review and verify to your own satisfaction the words of your sources. It would be wise to consider every article on the Internet as suspect unless you have accessed it through your library's databases. See pages 50–51 for guidelines on judging the value of Internet articles.

A research project requires you to bring outside sources into your paper, so it only makes sense to choose the most reliable and well-written sources that you can find. Your evaluation of source material should focus on the relevance of the source and how it conveys the idea that you are presenting. Thus, your task is twofold: (1) you must read and personally evaluate the sources for your own benefit as a writer, and (2) you must present them to your reader in your text as validated and authentic sources. This chapter offers a few tips on how to meet those two responsibilities.

6a Understanding the Assignment

A general search for sources on the Internet may serve your needs for writing a short paper, but the research paper requires you to compose from books, scholarly journals, and academic articles. Also, a specific academic discipline usually controls your research. For example, an assignment to examine the recreational programs at selected day-care centers will require research in the literature of the social sciences found in your library's electronic catalogs rather than on the Internet.

Primary and Secondary Sources

Primary sources are the original words of an authority. Original source material can be found in novels, speeches, eyewitness accounts, interviews, letters, autobiographies, observation during field research, or the written results of empirical research. You should feel free to quote often from a primary source that has direct relevance to your discussion. For example, if you present a poem by Dylan Thomas, you should quote the poem.

Secondary sources are writings about the primary sources, about an author, or about somebody's accomplishments. This type of material is a commentary about original, primary information. Secondary sources include a report on a presidential speech, a review of new scientific findings, analysis of a poem, or a biography of a notable person. These evaluations, analyses, or interpretations provide ways of looking at original, primary sources. Following is a guide to sources for the major disciplines.

Guide to Academic Sources

Humanities

Primary sources in literature and the fine arts are novels, poems, and plays, as well as films, paintings, music, and sculptures. Your task is to examine, interpret, and evaluate these original works. Researchers in history need to look at speeches, documents written by historic figures, and some government documents.

Secondary sources in the humanities are evaluations in journal articles and books, critical reviews, biographies, and history books.

Field research in the humanities will require interviews with an artist or government official, letters, e-mail surveys, online discussion groups, or the archival study of manuscripts.

Social Sciences

Primary sources in education, political science, psychology, and other fields include speeches, writings by presidents and others, documents recorded in the *Congressional Record*, reports and statistics of government agencies and departments, and papers at your state's archival library.

Secondary sources include books and articles on social, political, and psychological issues; analyses and evaluations in journal articles; discussions of the business world in newspapers, magazines, and journals; and—in general—anything written about key personalities, events, products, and primary documents.

Field research is most important in the social sciences and will consist of case studies, findings from surveys and questionnaires, tests and test data, interviews, and observation. In business reports, field research consists of market testing, drawings and designs, industrial research, letters, and interviews.

Sciences

Primary sources in the various sciences consist of the words and theories of various scientists discussing natural phenomena or offering their views on scientific issues, such as the words of Charles Darwin or Stephen Hawking. At the same time, journal articles that report on empirical research are considered primary material because they are original in their testing of a hypothesis.

Secondary sources in the sciences are not abundant. They appear generally as review articles that discuss the testing and experiments by different scientists; for example, the review of four or five articles on gene mutation.

Field research and laboratory testing are crucial to the sciences and provide the results of experiments, discoveries, tests, and observations.

6b Identifying Reliable Sources

The inverted pyramid to the right presents a progression of sources from excellent down to less reliable. The chart does not ask you to ignore or dismiss items at the bottom, such as popular magazines or e-mail discussion groups, but it lets you know when to feel confident and when to be on guard about the validity of the source.

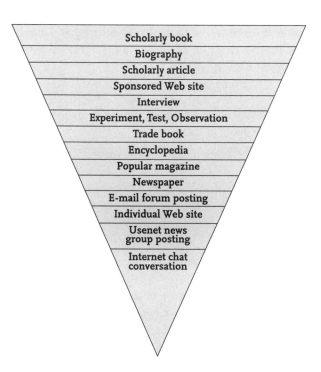

Scholarly Book

Scholarly books, including textbooks, treat academic topics with in-depth discussions and careful documentation of the evidence. A college library is a repository for scholarly books—technical and scientific works, doctoral dissertations, publications of the university presses, and many textbooks. Scholarly books are subjected to careful review before publication, and they are published because they give the very best treatment on a subject. However, in the sciences, books grow out-of-date quickly, so depend heavily upon monthly journals and updated Internet sites for current research.

Biography

The library's electronic catalog can help you find an appropriate biography from among the thousands available in such reference works as *Contemporary Authors* or *Dictionary of American Negro Biography*. You can also learn about a notable person on the Internet by using a search engine to search for the name of the person and carefully scanning the sites that are returned. Notable persons also have Web sites devoted to them. A *critical biography* is a book devoted not only to the life of one person but to the life's work of that person, such as Richard Ellmann's *Oscar Wilde*, which is a critical study of Wilde's writings as well as his life.

You may need a biography for several reasons:

- To verify the standing and reputation of somebody you want to paraphrase or quote in your paper.
- To provide biographical details in your introduction. For example, the primary topic may be Carl Jung's psychological theories of the unconscious, but some information about Jung's career might also be appropriate in the paper.
- To discuss a creative writer's life in relation to his or her work. That is, Joyce Carol Oates's personal life may shed some light on your reading of her stories or novels.

Scholarly Article

Scholarly articles are best found through one of the library's databases (see pages 21–27). The academic databases will take you to journal articles or articles at academically sponsored Web sites. You can be confident of the authenticity of journal articles because the authors document all sources, publish through university presses and academic organizations, and write for academic honor. Thus, a journal article about child abuse found in *Journal of Marriage and the Family* or found through the PsyINFO database may be considered reliable. You may also find well documented articles in respected periodicals, such as *Atlantic Monthly*, *Scientific Review*, and *Discover*. Major newspapers, such as the *New York Times*, *Atlanta Journal-Constitution*, and *Wall Street Journal*, also can be sources of valuable articles found in both printed and online editions.

Sponsored Web Site

The Internet supplies both excellent and dubious information. You must be careful when evaluating Web materials. Chapter 3 explores research on the Web. In addition to reviewing the "Evaluating Internet Sources" checklist on pages 50–51, you should ask yourself these questions about any Web site information:

- Is it appropriate to my work?
- Does it reveal a serious and scholarly emphasis?
- Is it sponsored by a professional institution or organization?

Interview

Interviews with knowledgeable people provide excellent information for a research paper. Whether conducted in person, by telephone, or by e-mail, the interview brings a personal, expert perspective into your work. The key element, of course, is the experience of the person. For full details about conducting an interview, see pages 54–55.

Experiment, Test, or Observation

Gathering your own data for research is a staple in many fields, especially the sciences. An experiment will bring primary evidence into your paper as you explain your hypothesis, give the test results, and discuss the implications of your findings. For details on the format for a scientific investigation, see pages 59–61.

Trade Book

Good to Great: Why Some Companies Make the Leap . . . and Others Don't and *A Field Guide to Industrial Relations* are typical titles of nonfiction trade books to be found in bookstores, not in a college library, although public libraries often have some holdings in trade books. Designed for commercial consumption, trade books seldom treat in-depth a scholarly subject. Unlike scholarly books and textbooks, most manuscripts for trade books do not go through the rigors of peer review. For example, if your topic is "dieting" with a focus on "fad diets," you will find plenty of diet books at the local book store and numerous articles on commercial Web sites. However, serious discussions of fad diets backed by careful research will be found in journals or sponsored Web sites.

Encyclopedia

An encyclopedia, by design, contains brief surveys of every well-known person, event, place, and accomplishment. You may read an encyclopedia essay when you begin investigating a topic, but most instructors will prefer that you go beyond encyclopedias to cite from scholarly books and journal articles. However, specialized encyclopedias (see pages 28–29) often have in-depth articles by noted scholars.

Popular Magazine

Like a trade book, a magazine article seldom offers in-depth information and does not face critical review of a panel of experts. Thus, you must exercise caution when using a magazine as a source. In general, college libraries have magazines containing high-quality writing, so depend on your library's list of periodicals when judging quality. For example, if your paper concerns sports medicine, citing an article from *Atlantic Monthly* or *Scientific Review* will gain you far higher marks than citing one from *Sports Illustrated, Sport,* or *NBA Basketball*.

Newspapers

Newspapers have reporters writing under the pressure of deadlines. They do not have as much time for the kind of careful research afforded writers of journal articles. On occasion, a newspaper will assign reporters to a series of articles on a complex topic, and such in-depth analyses have merit. The major print and online newspapers often hire highly qualified writers and columnists, so valuable articles can be found in these sources. Remember, however, that newspaper articles, like those in magazines and on the Internet, must be cautiously and critically evaluated.

E-mail Forum Posting

E-mail information via an e-mail forum established by the instructor for a course deserves consideration when it focuses on academic issues, such as "British Romantic literature," or more specifically "Shelley's poetry." In some cases, they originate for students in an online course, providing an avenue for sharing ideas. However, rather than search for quotable material from e-mail forums, use them as a sounding board to generate ideas and test them with other participants.

Individual Web Site

A person's home page, with its various links to other information, provides a publication medium for anybody who may or may not possess knowledge. You cannot avoid them, because they pop up on results lists of the search engines. You should approach them with caution. For example, one student, investigating the topic "fad diets" searched the Web to find mostly home pages that described personal battles with weight loss or commercial sites that were blatant in their attempts to sell something. Caution becomes vital.

Internet Chat Conversations

Real-time Internet conversations have almost no value for academic research and are not legitimate sources for your paper. Seldom do you know the participants beyond their usernames, and the conversations rarely focus on scholarly issues.

6c Evaluating Sources

Confronted by several books and articles, many writers have trouble determining the value of material and the contribution it will make to their research paper. To save time, you need to be selective in your reading. To serve your reader, you need to cite carefully selected material that is pertinent to your argument. Avoid dumping huge blocks of quotation into your paper, because doing so results in the loss of your style and voice. As you select, evaluate, and use research materials, you must be concerned about the relevance, authority, accuracy, and currency of all sources that you cite.

Relevance

To determine how well an article or book fits the demands of your research, first skim the material. For a periodical or Internet article, examine the title, the abstract or introduction, and both the opening and closing paragraphs.

Authority

To test the authority of a source, examine the credentials of the author (usually found in a brief biographical profile or professional affiliation blurb) and the sponsoring institution, which is usually the publisher of a journal, such as the American Sociological Association, or the sponsors of a Web site, such as the University of California, Los Angeles, of http://www.ucla.edu. Look at the bibliography at the end of the article, for it signals the scholarly nature of the work and points you toward other material on your subject. Study the home page of an Internet article, if there is one. Prefer sites sponsored by universities and professional organizations. Take note of hypertext links to other sites whose quality may be determined by the domain tags *.edu*, *.org*, and *.gov*. Be wary of *com* sites. See pages 50–51 for guidelines on judging the value of Internet articles.

Note: The **definitive edition** of a work is the most reliable version of a play, novel, or collection of poems because the definitive edition is one that the author supervised through the press. The way an author wanted to present the work can be found only in a definitive edition. Thus, electronic versions usually do not display the original author's page and type design, unless they are photocopies of the original, as with the JSTOR site (see page 24).

Accuracy

In the sciences, scholars talk about verification of an article, which means they can, if necessary, replicate the research and the findings described in the article. A scientific report must carefully detail the design of the work, as well as its methods, subjects, and procedures. A lab experiment, for example, should repeat previous findings to demonstrate accuracy. The writer should reveal the details of a control group, an experimental group, and the testing procedures. Any scientific report that does not establish research methods should not be cited.

Currency

Use recent sources for research in the sciences and social sciences. A psychology book may look valuable, but if its copyright date is 1955, the content probably is outdated and has been replaced by recent research and current developments. When reading a source, be certain that at least one date is listed. Electronic publications sometimes show the site has been updated or refreshed, but the article may carry an older date. On the Internet, check the date of print publication; it may be different from the Web publication. As a general rule, use the most recent date for an article on the Internet, which means you could list as many as three dates—the year of the print publication, the most recent year of the Internet publication, and the date you accessed the material.

CHAPTER 7

Organizing Ideas and Setting Goals

Initially, research is haphazard, and its results will clutter your work space with bits of information on notes and photocopied sheets. So, after investigating and gathering sufficient sources for your project, you need to organize the information to serve specific needs. The structure of your project becomes clear only when you organize your research materials into a proposal, a list of ideas, a set of questions, or a rough outline. In most cases, the design of your study should match an appropriate organizational model, sometimes called a **paradigm,** which means "an example that serves as a pattern or model." The organizational models in this chapter will help you organize your notes, photocopies, and downloaded files. Each scholarly field gives a special insight into any given topic, and each research assignment demands its own approaches which produce different kinds of papers in a variety of formats for the discipline involved. By following an academic model, you can ensure that your research project will have the correct design to meet the demands of the assignment.

7a Using the Correct Academic Model (Paradigm)

A traditional outline, because it is content specific, is useful for only one paper, while an academic pattern, such as those shown below, governs all papers within a certain design. For example, a general, all-purpose model gives a plan for almost any research topic.

A General, All-Purpose Model

If you are uncertain about your assignment, start with this basic model and expand it with your material to make it a detailed outline. It offers plenty of leeway. Readers, including your instructor, are accustomed to this sequence for research papers.

- Identify the subject in the *introduction*. Explain the problem, provide background information, and give a clear thesis statement.
- Analyze the subject in the *body* of the paper. You can compare, analyze, give evidence, trace historical events, and handle other matters.
- Discuss your findings in the *conclusion*. You can challenge an assumption, interpret the findings, provide solutions, or reaffirm your thesis.

The specific design of any model is based on the nature of the assignment and the discipline for which you are writing. Each of the following forms is explained below.

Academic Pattern for the Interpretation of Literature and Other Creative Works

If you plan to interpret a musical, artistic, or literary work, such as an opera, a set of paintings, or a novel, adjust this next model to your subject and purpose and build it, with your factual data, into a working outline:

Introduction
Identify the work.
Give a brief summary in one sentence.
Provide background information that relates to the thesis.
Offer biographical facts about the artist that relate to the specific issues.
Quote and paraphrase authorities to establish the scholarly traditions.
Write a thesis sentence that establishes your particular views of the literary work.
Body
Provide evaluative analysis divided by imagery, theme, design, use of color, character development, structure, symbolism, narration, language, musical themes, and so forth.

Conclusion

Keep a fundamental focus on the artist of the work, not just the elements of analysis as explained in the body.

Offer a conclusion that explores the contributions of the artist in accordance with your thesis sentence.

Academic Pattern for the Analysis of History

If you are writing a historical or political science paper that analyzes events and their causes and consequences, your paper should conform in general to the following plan. Flesh it out with the notes in your research journal to make it a working outline for drafting your paper.

Introduction

Identify the event.

Provide the background leading up to the event.

Offer quotations and paraphrases from experts.

Give the thesis sentence.

Body

Analyze the background leading up to the event.

Trace events from one historic episode to another.

Offer a chronological sequence that explains how one event relates directly to the next.

Cite authorities who have also investigated this event in history.

Conclusion

Reaffirm your thesis.

Discuss the consequences of this event.

Academic Pattern for Advancing Philosophical and Religious Ideas

If the assignment is to defend or analyze a topic from the history of ideas, use this next design, but adjust it as necessary. Make it your working outline by writing sentences and even paragraphs for each item in the model.

Introduction

Establish the idea or question.

Trace its history.

Discuss its significance.

Introduce experts who have addressed the idea.

Provide a thesis sentence that presents your approach to the issue(s), from a fresh perspective if at all possible.

Body

Evaluate the issues surrounding the concept.

Develop a past-to-present examination of theories.

Compare and analyze the details and minor issues.

Cite experts who have addressed this idea.

Conclusion

Advance and defend your thesis as it grows out of evidence about the idea.

Close with an effective quotation from a noted person.

Academic Pattern for the Review of a Performance

If the assignment asks you to review a musical, artistic, or literary performance, such as an opera, a set of paintings, a reading, a drama, or a theatrical performance, adjust this next paradigm to your subject and purpose. *Note:* The review differs with the interpretation (see page 80) by its focus on evaluation rather than on analysis.

Introduction

Identify the work.

Give a brief summary in one sentence.

Provide background information or history of the work.

Offer biographical facts about the artist that relate to the specific issues.

Quote and paraphrase authorities to establish the scholarly traditions that relate to this work and the performance.

Write a thesis sentence that establishes your judgment about the performance.

Body

Offer an evaluation as based upon a predetermined set of criteria. Judge a drama by its staging and acting, music by its quality of voice and instruments, art by its design, literature by its themes, and so forth.

Conclusion

Keep a fundamental focus on the performance, the performers, and the artist of the work.

Offer a judgment, as based on the criteria given in the body.

Academic Pattern for Advancing
Your Ideas and Theories

If you want to advance a social or legal theory in your paper, use this next design, but adjust it to eliminate some items and add new elements as necessary. Build this model into a working outline by assigning your notes, photocopies, and downloaded files to a specific line of the model.

Introduction
    Establish the theory, problem, or question.
    Discuss its significance.
    Provide the necessary background information.
    Introduce experts who have addressed the problem.
    Provide a thesis sentence that relates the problem to a fresh
        perspective.
Body
    Evaluate the issues involved in the problem.
    Develop a chronological examination.
    Compare and analyze the details and minor issues.
    Cite experts who have addressed the same problem.
Conclusion
    Advance and defend your theory.
    Discuss the implications of your findings.
    Offer directives or a plan of action.
    Suggest additional research that might be appropriate.

Academic Pattern for Argument
and Persuasion Papers

If you write persuasively or argue from a set position, your paper should conform in general to this next paradigm. Select the elements that fit your design, begin to elaborate on them, and gradually build a frame for your paper.

Introduction
    Establish clearly the problem or controversy that your paper will
        examine.
    Summarize the issues.
    Define key terminology.
    Make concessions on some points of the argument.
    Use quotations and paraphrases to explore the controversy.

Provide background information.

Write a thesis to establish your position.

Body

Develop arguments to defend one side of the subject.

Analyze the issues, both pro and con.

Give evidence from the sources, including quotations from the scholarship as appropriate.

Conclusion

Expand your thesis into a conclusion to demonstrate that your position has been formulated logically through careful analysis and discussion of the issues.

Academic Model for a Comparative Study

A comparative study requires that you examine two schools of thought, two issues, two works, or the positions taken by two persons. It explores similarities and differences, generally using one of three arrangements for the body of the paper. As you embellish the model, you will gradually build your working outline.

Introduction

Establish A.

Establish B.

Briefly compare the two.

Introduce the central issues.

Cite source materials on the subjects.

Present your thesis.

Body (choose one)

Examine A	Compare A & B	Issue 1: Discuss A & B
Examine B	Contrast A & B	Issue 2: Discuss A & B
Compare and	Discuss the	Issue 3: Discuss A & B
contrast A & B	central issues	

Conclusion

Discuss the significant issues.

Write a conclusion that ranks one over the other, or write a conclusion that rates the respective genius of each side.

Academic Pattern for a Laboratory Investigation or Field Report

This model is rigid with little flexibility. Instructors will expect your report to remain tightly focused on each of these items.

Introduction

Provide the title, the experiment number, and the date.

Describe the experiment.

List any literature consulted.

Objectively describe what it is that you hope to accomplish.

Method

Explain the procedures used to reproduce the experiment.

Explain the design of the test.

Identify any tools or apparatus used.

Identify any variables that affected your research (weather conditions, temperatures, and so on).

Results

Give your findings, including statistical data.

Discussion

Provide your interpretation of the data.

Discuss any implications to be drawn from the research.

Comment on what you learned by the experiment (optional).

Academic Pattern for Scientific Analysis

In this situation, you are working with the literature on a scientific issue, so you have more flexibility than with a report on a lab experiment.

Introduction

Identify the scientific issue, problem, and state your hypothesis.

Explore the history of the topic.

Cite the literature that pertains to the topic.

Explain the purpose of the examination and its possible implications.

Body

Classify the issues.

Analyze, define, and compare each aspect of the topic.

Offer cause/effect explanations.

Make a detailed inquiry into all relevant issues.

Conclusion

Explain the current findings of scientific studies related to your topic.

Advance your reasons for continued research.

Suggest possible findings.

Discuss the implications of your analysis.

Academic Pattern for a Report of Empirical Research

This pattern is similar to the one for a laboratory investigation, so follow it closely to fulfill all the required items.

Introduction
Present the point of your study.
State the hypothesis and how it relates to the problem.
Provide the theoretical implications.
Explain the manner in which your study relates to previously published work.
Method
Describe the subject (what was tested, who participated, whether the participants were human or animal, and where the field work was accomplished).
Describe the apparatus (explain what equipment you used and how you used it).
Summarize the procedure and the execution of each stage of your work.
Results
Summarize the data you collected.
Provide statistical treatment of your findings with tables, graphs, and charts.
Include findings that conflict with your hypothesis.
Discuss the implications of your work.
Evaluate the data and its relevance to the hypothesis.
Interpret the findings as necessary.
Discuss the implications of the findings.
Qualify the results and limit them to your specific study.
Make inferences from the results.
Suggest areas worthy of additional research.

7b Using Your Thesis to Control the Outline

After you have selected an academic pattern appropriate to your assignment, you should use your thesis statement (or hypothesis) to set the tone and direction of your paper. Notice in the following examples how variations in the thesis can affect the arrangement of the paper.

Argument

> **THESIS:** Misunderstandings about organ donation distort reality and set serious limits on the availability of organs for those persons who need an eye, a liver, or a healthy heart.
>
> **ARGUMENT 1.** Many myths mislead people into believing that donation is unethical.
>
> **ARGUMENT 2.** Some fear that as a patient they might be put down early.
>
> **ARGUMENT 3.** Religious views sometimes get in the way of donation.

This preliminary outline gives this writer three categories for an analysis of the issues.

Cause and Effect

> **THESIS:** Television can have positive effects on a child's language development.
>
> **CONSEQUENCE 1.** Television introduces new words.
>
> **CONSEQUENCE 2.** Television reinforces word usage and proper syntax.
>
> **CONSEQUENCE 3.** Literary classics come alive on television.
>
> **CONSEQUENCE 4.** Television exposes children to the subtle rhythms and musical effects of accomplished speakers.

Evaluation

> **THESIS:** The architectural drawing for the university's new student center shows the design is not friendly to people who are handicapped.
>
> **EVALUATION 1.** The common areas seem cramped and narrow, with few open areas in which students can cluster.
>
> **EVALUATION 2.** Steps and stairs seem all too common in the design.
>
> **EVALUATION 3.** Only one elevator appears in the plans when three would be fair and equitable.
>
> **EVALUATION 4.** Only the first-floor restrooms offer universal access.

The parking spaces designated for people with physical handicaps are located at an entrance with steps, not a ramp.

The outline evolves from a thesis statement that invites evaluation of an architectural plan.

Comparison

THESIS: Discipline often involves punishment, but child abuse adds another element: the gratification of the adult.

COMPARISON 1: A spanking has the interest of the child at heart, but a beating or a caning has no redeeming value.

COMPARISON 2: Time-outs remind the child that relationships are important and to be cherished, but lock-outs in a closet only promote hysteria and fear.

COMPARISON 3: The parent's ego and selfish interests often take precedence over the welfare of the child or children.

This outline provides a pattern of comparison by which to judge the relative differences between punishment of a child and child abuse.

7c Writing an Outline

Not all papers require a complete, formal outline, nor do all researchers need one. A short research paper can be created from key words, a list of issues, a rough outline, and a first draft. Creating a formal outline can be worthwhile, however, for it fleshes out the academic pattern you have selected (see 7a) by classifying the issues of your study into clear, logical categories with main headings and one or more levels of subheadings.

A formal outline is not rigid and inflexible; you may, and should, modify it while writing and revising. In every case, treat an outline or organizational chart as a tool. Like an architect's blueprint, it should contribute to, not inhibit, the construction of a finished product. You may wish to experiment with the "outline" feature of your software, which allows you to view the paper at various levels of detail and to highlight and "drop" the essay into a different organization.

Topic Outline

Build a topic outline of balanced phrases. You can use noun phrases ("the rods of the retina"), gerund phrases ("sensing dim light with retina rods"), or infinitive phrases ("to sense dim light with retina rods"). No matter which grammatical format you choose, follow it consistently throughout the outline. One student used noun phrases to outline her scientific analysis:

I. Diabetes defined
   A. A disease without control
      1. A disorder of the metabolism
      2. The search for a cure
   B. Types of diabetes
      1. Type 1, juvenile diabetes
      2. Type 2, adult onset diabetes
II. Health complications
   A. The problem of hyperglycemia
      1. Signs and symptoms of the problem
      2. Lack of insulin
   B. The conflict of the kidneys and the liver
      1. Effects of ketoacidosis
      2. Effects of arteriosclerosis
III. Proper care and control
   A. Blood sugar monitoring
      1. Daily monitoring at home
      2. Hemoglobin test at a laboratory
   B. Medication for diabetes
      1. Insulin injections
      2. Hypoglycemia agents
   C. Exercise programs
      1. Walking
      2. Swimming
      3. Aerobic workouts
   D. Diet and meal planning
      1. Exchange plan
      2. Carbohydrate counting
IV. Conclusion: Balance of all the factors

Sentence Outline

In contrast to an outline with phrases, you may use full sentences for each heading and subheading. Using sentences has two advantages over the topic outline: (1) many entries in a sentence outline can serve as topic sentences for paragraphs, thereby accelerating the writing process, and (2) the subject-verb pattern establishes the logical direction of your thinking (for example, the phrase *Vocabulary development* becomes *Television viewing can improve a child's vocabulary*). Note below a brief portion of one student's sentence outline.

I. Organ and tissue donation is the gift of life.
   A. Organs that can be successfully transplanted include the heart, lungs, liver, kidneys, and pancreas.
   B. Tissues that can be transplanted successfully include bone, corneas, skin, heart valves, veins, cartilage, and other connective tissues.
   C. The process of becoming a donor is easy.
   D. Many people receive organ and tissue transplants each year, but still many people die because they did not receive the needed transplant.

CHAPTER 8

Writing Effective Notes

Note taking is the heart of research. If you write high-quality notes, they may need only minor editing to fit into the appropriate places in your first draft. Prepare yourself to write different types of notes—quotations for well-phrased passages by authorities but also paraphrased or summarized notes to maintain your voice. This chapter explains the following types of notes:

- *Personal notes* that express your own ideas or record field research
- *Quotation notes* that preserve any distinguished syntax of an authority
- *Paraphrase notes* that interpret and restate what the authority has said
- *Summary notes* that capture in capsule form a writer's ideas
- *Field notes* that record interviews, tabulate questionnaires, and maintain records of laboratory experiments and other types of field research

Honoring the Conventions of Research Style

Your note taking will be more effective from the start if you practice the conventions of style for citing a source within your text.

MLA: Lawrence Smith states, "The suicidal teen causes severe damage to the psychological condition of peers" (34).

APA: Smith (2009) stated , "The suicidal teen causes severe damage to the psychological condition of peers" (p. 34).

CMS footnote: Lawrence Smith explains , "The suicidal teen causes severe damage to the psychological condition of peers."[3]

CSE number: Smith (4) said , "The suicidal teen causes severe damage to the psychological condition of peers."

The MLA style is the default style displayed throughout this chapter.

CHECKLIST: Writing Effective Notes

1. Whether you are using a research journal or your computer's word processor, create a separate, labeled file within a project folder for each note topic or source. Keep notes and downloaded materials in the files.
2. Include the name, year, and page of all sources in order to prepare for creating in-text citations.
3. Label each file (for example, "objectivity on television").
4. Write a full note in well-developed sentences to speed the writing of your first draft.
5. Keep everything (photocopy, scribbled note) in order to authenticate dates, page numbers, or full names.
6. Label your personal notes with "my idea" or "personal note" to distinguish them from the sources.

8a Writing Personal Notes

The content of a research paper is an expression of your own ideas as supported by scholarly evidence. It is not a collection of ideas transmitted by experts in books and articles. Readers are primarily interested in *your* thesis statement, *your* topic sentences, and *your* personal view of the issues. Therefore, during your research, record your thoughts on the issues by writing plenty of personal notes in your research journal and computer files. Personal notes are essential because they allow you to record your discoveries, reflect on the findings, make connections, and identify the prevailing views and patterns of thought. Remember two standards: (1) the idea written into the file is yours, and (2) the file is labeled with "my idea," "mine," or "personal thought" to distinguish it from information borrowed from a source.

Here is an example:

Personal thought

    For me, organ donation might be a gift of life, so I have signed
my donor card. At least a part of me will continue to live if an accident
claims my life. My boyfriend says I'm gruesome, but I consider it practical.
Besides, he might be the one who benefits, and then what will he say?

8b Writing Direct Quotation Notes

Quotation notes are essential because they allow you to capture the
authoritative voices of the experts on the topic, feature well-phrased
statements, offer conflicting points of view, and share the literature on
the topic with your readers. Follow these basic conventions.

1. Select material that is important and well-phrased, not some-
   thing trivial or something that is common knowledge. NOT
   "John F. Kennedy was a Democrat from Massachusetts"
   (Rupert 233) but this:

   > "John F. Kennedy's Peace Corps left a legacy of lasting compassion
   > for the downtrodden"(Rupert 233).

2. Use quotation marks around the quoted material in your notes,
   working draft, and final manuscript. Do not copy or download
   the words of a source into your paper in such a way that readers
   will think that *you* wrote the material.
3. Use the exact words of the source.
4. Provide an appropriate in-text citation, as shown by this note:

   > Griffiths, Kilman, and Frost suggest that the killing of architect Stanford
   > White in 1904 was "the beginning of the most bitterly savage century
   > known to mankind" (113). Murder, wars, and human atrocities were the
   > "sad vestiges" of an era that had great promise.

5. The parenthetical citation goes *outside* the final quotation mark but
   inside the period for quotations run on within your sentence. Block
   quotations require a different setup (see pages 96–97).
6. Quote key sentences and short passages, not entire paragraphs.
   Find the essential statement and feature it; do not force your
   reader to read a long quoted passage that has only one statement

relevant to your point. Make the essential idea a part of your sentence, as shown here:

> Many Americans, trying to mend their past eating habits, adopt functional foods as an essential step toward a more health-conscious future. Balthrop says this group of believers spends "an estimated $29 billion a year" on functional foods (6).

7. Quote from both primary sources (the original words by a writer or speaker) and secondary sources (the comments after the fact about original works). The two types are discussed immediately below.

Quoting the Primary Sources

Quote from primary sources for four specific reasons:

- To draw on the wisdom of the original author.
- To let readers hear the precise words of the original author.
- To copy exact lines of poetry and drama.
- To reproduce graphs, charts, and statistical data.

Cite poetry, fiction, drama, letters, and interviews. In other cases, you may want to quote liberally from a presidential speech, cite the words of a businessman, or reproduce original data.

Quoting the Secondary Sources

Quote from secondary sources for three specific reasons:

- To display excellence in ideas and expression by experts on the topic.
- To explain complex material.
- To set up a statement of your own, especially if it spins off, adds to, or takes exception to the source as quoted.

The overuse of direct quotation from secondary sources indicates that either you: (1) did not have a clear focus and copied verbatim just about everything related to the subject, or (2) had inadequate evidence and used numerous quotations as padding. Therefore, limit quotations from secondary sources by using only a phrase or a sentence:

> Reginald Herman says the geographical changes in Russia require "intensive political analysis" (15).

If you quote an entire sentence, make the quotation a direct object. It tells *what* the authority says.

> In response to the changes in Russia, one critic notes, "The American government must exercise caution and conduct intensive political analysis" (15).

8c Writing Paraphrased Notes

A paraphrase requires you to restate in your own words the thought, meaning, and attitude of someone else. Your interpretation acts as a bridge between the source and the reader as you capture the wisdom of the source in approximately the same number of words. Use paraphrase to maintain your voice or style in the paper, to avoid an endless string of direct quotations, and to interpret the source as you rewrite it. Keep in mind these five rules for paraphrasing a source:

1. Rewrite the original in about the same number of words.
2. Provide an in-text citation to the source (the author and page number in MLA style).
3. Retain exceptional words and phrases from the original by enclosing them within quotation marks.
4. Preserve the tone of the original by suggesting moods of satire, anger, humor, doubt, and so on. Show the author's attitude with appropriate verbs: "Omar Tavares condemns . . . defends . . . argues . . . explains . . . observes . . . defines."
5. Put the original aside while paraphrasing to avoid copying word for word. Compare the finished paraphrase with the original source to be certain that the paraphrase truly rewrites the original and that it uses quotation marks with any phrasing or key words retained from the original.

HINT

When instructors see an in-text citation but no quotations marks, they will assume that you are paraphrasing, not quoting. Be sure that their assumption is true.

Here are examples that show the differences between a quotation note and a paraphrased one:

Quotation:

Hein explains heredity in this way: "Except for identical twins, each person's heredity is unique" (294).

Paraphrase:

One source explains that heredity is special and distinct for each of us, unless a person is one of identical twins (Hein 294).

Quotation (block indent if four lines or more):

Hein explains the phenomenon in this way:

> Since only half of each parent's chromosomes are transmitted
> to a child and since this half represents a chance selection
> of those the child could inherit, only twins that develop
> from a single fertilized egg that splits in two have identical
> chromosomes. (294)

Paraphrase:

Hein specifies that twins have identical chromosomes because they grow from one egg that divides after it has been fertilized. He affirms that most brothers and sisters differ because of the "chance selection" of chromosomes transmitted by each parent (294).

As shown in the example immediately above, place any key wording of the source within quotation marks.

8d Writing Summary Notes

A summary of a source captures in just a few words the ideas of an entire paragraph, section, or chapter. It may be a rough sketch of the source or a polished note. Store each summary in your project folder with its own file name. Use a summary for these reasons:

- To review an article or book.
- To annotate a bibliography entry.
- To provide a plot summary.
- To create an abstract.

Success with the summary requires you do the following:

1. Condense the original content with precision and directness. Reduce a long paragraph into a sentence, tighten an article into a brief paragraph, and summarize a book into a page.
2. Preserve the tone of the original. If the original is serious, suggest that tone in the summary. In the same way, retain moods of doubt, skepticism, optimism, and so forth.
3. Write the summary in your own language; however, retain exceptional phrases from the original, enclosing them in quotation marks.
4. Provide documentation.

Use the Summary to Review Briefly an Article or Book

Note this example that reviews two entire articles:

Alec Twobears has two closely related articles on this subject, and both, one in 2005 and another in 2006, are about the failure of the United States to follow through with the treaties it signed with the Indian nations of North America. He opens both with "No treaty is a good treaty!" He signals clearly the absence of trust by Native Americans toward the government in Washington, DC.

To see more summaries of this type, presented in a review of the literature, see pages 101–109.

Use the Summary to Write an Annotated Bibliography

An annotation offers a brief explanation or critical commentary on an article or book. Thus, an annotated bibliography is one that cites a source followed immediately by the annotation, as shown here in MLA style.

"Top Ten Myths about Donation and Transplantation." TransWeb Webcast. 30 Sept. 2008. Web. 9 Oct. 2009. This site dispels the many myths surrounding organ donation, showing that selling organs is illegal, that matching donor and recipient is highly complicated, and that secret back room operations are almost impossible.

See pages 99–101 to view more annotated bibliography entries.

Use the Summary in a Plot Summary Note

In just a few sentences a summary can describe a novel, short story, drama, or similar literary work, as shown by this next note:

Great Expectations by Dickens describes young Pip, who inherits money and can live the life of a gentleman. But he discovers that his "great expectations" have come from a criminal. With that knowledge his attitude changes from one of vanity to one of compassion.

Use the Summary to Create an Abstract

An abstract is a brief description that appears at the beginning of an article to summarize the contents. Usually, it is written by the article's author, and it helps readers make decisions about reading the entire article. You can find entire volumes devoted to abstracts, such as *Psychological Abstracts* or *Abstracts of English Studies*. An abstract is required for most papers in the social and natural sciences. Here is a sample from one student's paper:

Abstract

Functional foods, products that provide benefits beyond basic nutrition, are adding billions to the nation's economy each year. Functional foods are suspected to be a form of preventive medicine. Consumers hope that functional foods can calm some of their medical anxieties, while researchers believe that functional foods may lower health care costs. The paper identifies several functional foods, locates the components that make them work, and explains the role that each plays on the body.

8e Writing Notes from Field Research

For some research projects, you will be expected to conduct field research. This work may require you to record your notes on charts, on cards, on notepads, on laboratory notebooks, in a research journal, or on the computer. **Interviews** require careful note taking during the session and dutiful transcription of those notes to your draft. A tape recorder can serve as a backup to your note taking. A **questionnaire** produces valuable data for developing notes and graphs and charts for your research paper.

The procedures and findings of **experiments, tests, and measurements** serve as your notes for the "method" and "results" section of the report. Here is an example of one student's laboratory notebook containing a passage that he might transfer to the "procedures" section of his paper:

First, 25.0 ml of a vinegar sample was delivered to a 50-ml volumetric flask, with a 25-ml pipet, and diluted to the mark with distilled water. It was mixed thoroughly and 50-ml aliquot were emptied into three 250-ml conical flasks, with a 25-ml pipet, 50 ml of distilled water, and two drops of phenolphthalein were added to each of the flasks. The samples were then titrated with a .345 M NaOH solution until the first permanent pink color.

8f Using Your Notes to Write an Annotated Bibliography

Writing an annotated bibliography may appear as busywork, but it helps you evaluate the strength and nature of your sources. The annotated bibliography that follows is written in MLA style. An *annotation* is a summary of the contents of a book or article. A *bibliography* is a list of sources on a selected topic. Thus, an annotated bibliography does two important things: (1) it is a bibliographic list of a selection of sources, and (2) it summarizes the contents of each book or article.

The annotated bibliography below provides a summary of a few sources on the issues of tanning, tanning beds, lotions, and the dangers of skin cancer.

Delgado 1

Norman Delgado

Professor Frew

English 1020

24 January 2010

Annotated Bibliography

Cohen, Russell. "Tanning Trouble: Teens Are Using Tanning Beds in Record

Numbers." *Scholastic Choices* 18 (2003): 23–28. Print. Cohen warns

that tanning beds "can be just as dangerous as the sun's rays" (23).

The writer explains that tanning salons are not well regulated, so the

Each entry gives full bibliographic information on the source—author, title, and publication data—as well as a brief description of the article or book.

amount of exposure can be really dangerous. The writer also explains how skin type affects tanning and the dangers of cancer.

Conforth, Tracee. "Tanning Booths: Are They Worth the Risk?" *Women's Health*. 8 Dec. 2003. Web. 17 Jan. 2010. This site raises the central question of whether tanning booths are less dangerous than the sun. Most lay people agree that solar radiation is damaging to our skin. The fact is that they expect their skin to pass through these damaging changes. For these individuals, a deep, golden glow offsets the risk of skin cancer.

Geller, Alan C., et al. "Use of Sunscreen, Sunburning Rates, and Tanning Bed Use among More Than 10,000 U.S. Children and Adolescents." *Pediatrics* 109 (2002): 1009–15. Print. The objective of this study was to examine the psychosocial variables associated with teens seeking suntans. It collected data from questionnaires submitted by 10,079 boys and girls 12 to 18 years old. It concluded that many children are at risk for skin cancer because of failure to use sunscreen.

"Skin Care for Your Skin Type." Harvard Medical School. 24. June 2008. Web. 18 Jan. 2010. This site features Harvard Medical School's Consumer Health Information. In this article, information is given about the three main types of skin cancers as well as advice about tanning, including the use of sunscreen of SPF 15 or higher, use of suntan lotions, the effects of the sun, and the dangers of skin cancer.

"Skin Protection—My Teen Likes to Tan." St. Louis Children's Hospital. Mar. 2009. Web. 17 Jan. 2010. This site quotes Susan Mallory, the director of dermatology at St. Louis Children's Hospital, and Registered Nurse Ann Leonard, who both offer warning against the use of tanning beds. Rather than damaging the skin with sun or tanning beds, the two experts suggest the use of tanning sprays or lotions.

"Sunny Days." *Health Watch*. The U of Texas Southwestern Medical Center at Dallas. 2009. Web. 21 Jan. 2010. This article warns against sun worship and skipping sunscreen. Experts suggest more public education and warnings, for tanning damages the structure of the skin and promotes sagging skin and wrinkles in later life. Dr. Sarah Weitzul, a UT Southwestern dermatologist, says proper sunscreen use is the key to saving your skin from the sun.

Zazinski, Janic. "Melanoma: An Equal-opportunity Killer." *Research Briefs*. Boston U. 15 May 2003. Web. 18 Jan. 2010. This article cites Dr. Marie-France Demierre, a professor of dermatology, who laments the use of tanning beds by young women. In truth, women are joining men in contracting and dying of melanoma, in great part because of tanning beds. Demierre and Zazinski warn youngsters against addiction to tanning beds and sun worship.

8g Using Your Notes to Write a Review of the Literature

A review of literature presents a set of summaries in essay form. It has two purposes:

1. It helps you investigate the topic because it forces you to examine and then evaluate how each source addresses the problem.
2. It organizes and classifies the sources in some reasonable manner for the benefit of the reader.

Thus, you should relate each source to your central subject, and you should group the sources according to their support of your thesis. For example, the brief review that follows explores the literature on the subject of gender communication. It classifies the sources under a progression of headings: the issues, the causes (both environmental and biological), the consequences for both men and women, and possible solutions.

You also will need to arrange the sources according to your selected categories or to fit your preliminary outline. Sometimes it might be as simple as grouping those sources that favor a course of action and those that oppose it. In other cases you may need to summarize sources that examine different characters or elements.

Like Kaci Holz in the paper below, you may wish to use headings that identify your various sections.

Holz 1

Kaci Holz

Dr. Ruis

April 23, 2009

English 1010

The review of literature is an essay on the articles and books that address the writer's topic.

Gender Communication: A Review of the Literature

Several theories exist about different male and female communication styles. These ideas have been categorized below to establish the issues, show causes for communication failures and the consequences for both men and women, and suggest possible solutions.

The Issues

The writer uses the sources to establish the issues.

Deborah Tannen, Ph.D., is a professor of sociolinguistics at Georgetown University. In her book *You Just Don't Understand: Men and Women in Conversation,* 2001, she claims there are basic gender patterns or stereotypes that can be found. Tannen says that men participate in conversations to establish "a hierarchical social order," while women most often participate in conversations to establish "a network of connections" (Tannen, *Don't Understand* 24–25). She distinguishes between the way women use "rapport-talk" and the way men use "report-talk" (74).

In similar fashion, Susan Basow and Kimberly Rubenfeld in "'Troubles Talk': Effects of Gender and Gender Typing," explore in detail the sex roles and how they determine and often control the speech of each gender. They notice that "women may engage in 'troubles talk' to enhance communication; men may avoid such talk to enhance autonomy and dominance" (186).

In addition, Kawa Patel asserts that men and women "use conversation for quite different purposes." He provides a "no" answer to the question in his title, "Do Men and Women Speak the Same Language?" He claims that women converse to develop and maintain connections, while men converse to claim their position in the hierarchy they see around them. Patel asserts that women are less likely to speak publicly than are men because women often perceive such speaking as putting oneself on display. A man, on the other hand, is usually comfortable with speaking publicly because that is how he establishes his status among others (Patel).

Similarly, masculine people are "less likely than androgynous individuals to feel grateful for advice" (Basow and Rubenfeld 186).

Julia T. Wood's book *Gendered Lives* claims that "male communication is characterized by assertion, independence, competitiveness, and confidence [while] female communication is characterized by deference, inclusivity, collaboration, and cooperation" (440). This list of differences describes why men and women have such opposing communication styles.

In another book, Tannen addresses the issue that boys, or men, "are more likely to take an oppositional stance toward other people and the world" and "are more likely to find opposition entertaining—to enjoy watching a good fight, or having one" (Tannen, *Argument* 166). Girls try to avoid fights.

Causes

Two different theories suggest causes for gender differences—the environment and biology.

<u>Environmental Causes</u>. Tammy James and Bethann Cinelli mention, "The way men and women are raised contributes to differences in conversation and communication . . ." (41).

The writer now uses the sources to explain the causes for communication failures. Another author, Susan Witt, in "Parental Influence on Children's Socialization to Gender Roles," discusses the various findings that support the idea that parents have a great influence on their children during the development of their self-concept. She states, "Children learn at a very early age what it means to be a boy or a girl in our society" (253). She says that parents "[dress] infants in gender-specific colors, [give] gender-differentiated toys, and [expect] different behavior from boys and girls" (Witt 254).

Patel notices a cultural gap, defining culture as "shared meaning." He goes on to comment that problems come about because one spouse enters marriage with a different set of "shared meanings" than the other. The cultural gap affects the children. Patel also talks about the

"Battle of the Sexes" as seen in conflict between men and women. Reverting back to his "childhood gender pattern" theory, Patel claims, "Men, who grew up in a hierarchical environment, are accustomed to conflict. Women, concerned more with relationship and connection, prefer the role of peacemaker."

Like Patel, Deborah Tannen also addresses the fact that men and women often come from different worlds and different influences. She says, "Even if they grow up in the same neighborhood, on the same block, or in the same house, girls and boys grow up in different worlds of words" (Tannen, *Don't Understand* 43).

Biological Causes. Though Tannen often addresses the environmental issue in much of her research, she also looks at the biological issue in her book *The Argument Culture*. Tannen states, "Surely a biological component plays a part in the greater use of antagonism among men, but cultural influence can override biological inheritance" (Tannen, *Argument* 205). She sums up the nature versus nurture issue by saying, "The patterns that typify women's and men's styles of opposition and conflict are the result of both biology and culture" (207).

Lillian Glass, another linguistics researcher, has a 1992 book called *He Says, She Says: Closing the Communication Gap Between the Sexes*. Glass addresses the issue that different hormones found in men and women's bodies make them act differently and therefore communicate differently. She also discusses how brain development has been found to relate to sex differences.

Judy Mann says, "Most experts now believe that what happens to boys and girls is a complex interaction between slight biological differences and tremendously powerful social forces that begin to manifest themselves the minute the parents find out whether they are going to have a boy or a girl" (qtd. in McCluskey 6).

The writer now uses the sources to explain the consequences of communi-cation failures on both men and women.

Consequences of Gender Differences

Now that we have looked at different styles of gender communication and possible causes of gender communication, let us look at the possible results. Morgan and Coleman relate that divorce is one of the most stressful events a person can experience. They expound upon this point by stating, "The decision to divorce is typically made with ambivalence, uncertainty and confusion. It is a difficult step. The family identity changes, and the identities of the individuals involved change as well."

Through various studies, Deborah Tannen has concluded that men and women have different purposes for engaging in communication. In the open forum that Tannen led in 2004 (published on compact disc), she explains the different ways men and women handle communication throughout the day. She explains that a man constantly talks during his workday in order to impress those around him and to establish his status in the office. At home he wants peace and quiet. On the other hand, a woman is constantly cautious and guarded about what she says during her workday. Women try hard to avoid confrontation and avoid offending anyone with their language. So when a woman comes home from work she expects to be able to talk freely without having to guard her words. The consequence? The woman expects conversation, but the man is tired of talking (Tannen, *He Said*).

Solutions

Answers for better gender communication seem elusive. What can *The writer now depends on the sources to provide possible solutions.* be done about this apparent gap in communication between genders? In his article published in *Leadership*, Jeffrey Arthurs offers the obvious suggestion that women should make an attempt to understand the male model of communication and that men should make an attempt to understand the female model of communication.

However, in his article "Speaking Across the Gender Gap," David Cohen mentions that experts didn't think it would be helpful to teach men to communicate more like women and women to communicate more like men. This attempt would prove unproductive because it would go against what men and women have been taught since birth. Rather than change the genders to be more like one another, we could simply try to "understand" each other better.

In addition, Carolyn Crozier makes this observation, "The idea that women should translate their experiences into the male code in order to express themselves effectively . . . is an outmoded, inconsistent, subservient notion that should no longer be given credibility in modern society." She suggests three things we can change: 1) Change the norm by which leadership success is judged; 2) redefine what we mean by power; and 3) become more sensitive to the places and times when inequity and inequality occur (Crozier). Similarly, Patel offers advice to help combat "cross-cultural" fights. He suggests: 1) Identify your fighting style; 2) agree on rules of engagement; and 3) identify the real issue behind the conflict.

McCluskey claims men and women need honest communication that shows respect, and they must "manage conflict in a way that maintains the relationship and gets the job done" (5). She says, "To improve relationships and interactions between men and women, we must acknowledge the differences that do exist, understand how they develop, and discard dogma about what are the 'right' roles of women and men" (5).

Obviously, differences exist in the way men and women communicate, whether caused by biological and/or environmental factors. We can consider the possible causes, the consequences, and possible solutions. Using this knowledge, we should be able to more accurately interpret communication between the genders.

The separate Works Cited page gives full information on each source cited in the paper.

Works Cited

Arthurs, Jeffrey. "He Said, She Heard: Any Time You Speak to Both Men and Women, You're Facing Cross-Cultural Communication." *Leadership* 23.1 (Winter 2002): 49. *Expanded Academic*. Web. 19 Apr. 2009.

Basow, Susan A., and Kimberly Rubenfeld. "'Troubles Talk': Effects of Gender and Gender Typing." *Sex Roles: A Journal of Research* (2003): 183–186. *Expanded Academic*. Web. 19 Apr. 2009.

Cohen, David. "Speaking Across the Gender Gap." *New Scientist* 131.1783 (1991): 36. *Expanded Academic*. Web. 18 Apr. 2009.

Crozier, Carolyn Y. "Subservient Speech: Women Need to be Heard."

8 Aug. 2008. Web. 15 Apr. 2009.

Glass, Lillian. *He Says, She Says: Closing the Communication Gap*

Between the Sexes. New York: G. P. Putnam's Sons, 1992. Print.

James, Tammy, and Bethann Cinelli. "Exploring Gender-Based

Communication Styles." *Journal of School Health* 73 (2003):

41–42. Print.

McCluskey, Karen Curnow. "Gender at Work." *Public Management*

79.5 (1997): 5–10. Print.

Morgan, Marni, and Marilyn Coleman. "Focus on Families: Divorce

and Adults." 12 Aug. 2005. Web. 17 Apr. 2009.

Patel, Kawa. "Do Men and Women Speak the Same Language?"

14 Nov. 2008. Web. 18 Apr. 2009.

Tannen, Deborah. *The Argument Culture: Moving from Debate*

to Dialogue. New York: Random House, 1998. Print.

---. *He Said, She Said: Exploring the Different Ways Men and Women*

Communicate. Print. New York: Barnes & Noble, 2004. CD.

---. *You Just Don't Understand: Women and Men in Conversation*.

New York: HarperCollins, 2001. Print.

Witt, Susan D. "Parental Influence on Children's Socialization

to Gender Roles." *Adolescence* 32 (1997): 253. Print.

Woods, Julia T. *Gendered Lives*. 6th ed. San Francisco: Wadsworth,

2004. Print.

Drafting the Paper in an Academic Style

As you draft your paper, your voice should flow from one idea to the next smoothly and logically. Moreover, you should adopt an academic style that presents a fair, balanced treatment of the subject. Mentioning opposing viewpoints early in a report gives you something to work against and may strengthen your conclusion. Keep in mind negative findings because they have value and should be reported even if they contradict your original hypothesis (see pages 114–116 for more on the logic and ethics of a presentation).

Three principles for drafting may serve your needs:

- *Be practical.* Write portions of the paper when you are ready, skipping over sections of your outline that need more research or thought. Leave plenty of space for notes and corrections.
- *Be uninhibited.* Write without fear or delay because initial drafts are attempts to get words on the page rather than to create a polished document.
- *Be conscientious about citations.* Cite the names of the sources in your notes and text, enclose quotations, and preserve page numbers for the sources.

Your research project should examine a subject in depth and also examine *your* knowledge and the strength of *your* evidence. This chapter will help you find the style necessary for your field of study, to focus your argument, and to build the introduction, body, and conclusion.

9a Writing for Your Field of Study

Each discipline has its own special language, style of expression, and manuscript format. In time, you will learn fully the style for your college major, for there are distinctions in the writing styles for papers in the humanities, the social sciences, and the physical sciences.

Academic Style in the Humanities

Writing in one of the humanities will require you to adopt a certain style, as shown in the following example:

> Organ and tissue donation is the gift of life. Each year many people confront health problems due to diseases or congenital birth defects. Tom Taddonia explains that tissues such as skin, veins, and valves can be used to correct congenital defects, blindness, visual impairment, trauma, burns, dental defects, arthritis, cancer, vascular and heart disease (34). Steve Barnill says, "More than 400 people each month receive the gift of sight through yet another type of tissue donation—corneal transplants. In many cases, donors unsuitable for organ donation are eligible for tissue donation." Barnill notes that tissues are now used in orthopedic surgery, cardiovascular surgery, plastic surgery, dentistry, and podiatry. Even so, not enough people are willing to donate organs and tissues.

Writing in the humanities is often concerned with the quality of life, of art, and of ideas, and has the following traits:

- Use of the present tense to indicate that this problem is an enduring one for humans of past ages as well as the present and the future
- Use of MLA style
- Discussion of theory as supported by the literature

Academic Style in the Social Sciences

A social science student, using APA style, might write the same passage as shown:

> Organ and tissue donation has been identified as a social as well as medical problem in the United States. On one side, people have confronted serious problems in securing organs and tissue to correct health problems; on the other, people have demonstrated a reluctance to donate their organs. This need has been identified by Taddonia (2010), Barnill (2007), Ruskin (2008),

and others. This hypothesis remains: People are reluctant to sign the donor cards. Consequently, this study will survey a random set of 1,000 persons who have drivers' licenses. The tabulations will indicate reasons for signing or not signing for donation. Further investigation can then be conducted to determine ways of increasing participation by potential donors.

With an objective approach to the topic, writing in the social sciences displays these characteristics:

- A scientific plan for examining a hypothesis
- Preference for the passive voice
- Minimal quotations from the sources, anticipating that readers will examine the literature for themselves
- An indication of the study's purpose and/or a general plan for empirical research
- Use of APA style for documenting the sources
- Use of past tense or the present perfect tense in references to the source material
- Awareness that this research will prompt further study

Academic Style in the Physical and Medical Sciences

A medical student might write on this same topic, as shown in CSE number style:

Taddonia (1) has shown that human tissue can be used to correct many defects. Barnill (2) showed that more than 400 people receive corneal transplants each month. Yet the health profession needs more donors. It has been shown (3–6) that advanced care directives by patients with terminal illnesses would improve the donation of organs and tissue and relieve relatives of making any decision. Patients have been encouraged to complete organ donation cards (7) as well as to sign living wills (5, 8), special powers of attorney (5), and DNR (do not resuscitate) orders (5, 8). It is encouraged that advanced care directives become standard for the terminally ill.

Scientific writing, like the passage above, typically features some of these traits:

- An objective approach to the topic without signs of personal commitment
- A search for a professional position (i.e., on organ donation)
- A preference for the passive voice and for past tense verbs

- A preference for the CSE citation-sequence system or, in some cases, the name-year system (see the example above)
- A reluctance to quote from the sources

9b Focusing Your Argument

Your writing style in the research paper needs to be factual, but it should also reflect your ideas on the topic. You will be able to draft your paper more quickly if you focus on the key issue(s). Each paragraph should build on and amplify your primary claim.

Persuading, Inquiring, and Negotiating

Establishing a purpose for writing is one way to focus your argument. Do you wish to persuade, inquire, or negotiate? Most research papers make an inquiry.

Persuasion means that you wish to convince the reader that your position is valid and, perhaps, to take action. For example:

Research has shown that homeowners and wild animals cannot live together in harmony. Thus, we need to establish green zones in every city of this country to control the sprawl in urban areas and to protect a segment of the natural habitat for the animals.

Inquiry is an exploratory approach to a problem in which you examine the issues without the insistence of persuasion. It is a truth-seeking adventure. You will often need to examine, test, or observe in order to discuss the implications of the research. For example:

Many suburban homedwellers complain that deer, raccoons, and other wild animals ravage their gardens, flowerbeds, and garbage cans; however, the animals were there first. Thus, we need a task force to examine the rights of each side in this conflict.

Negotiation is a search for a solution. It means that you attempt to resolve a conflict by inventing options or a mediated solution. For example:

Suburban neighbors need to find ways to embrace the wild animals that have been displaced rather than voice anger at the animals or the county government. Research has shown that green zones and wilderness trails would solve some of the problems; however, such a solution would require serious negotiations with real estate developers who want to use every square foot of every development.

Maintaining a Focus with Ethical and Logical Appeals

As an objective writer, you will need to examine the problem, make your claim, and provide supporting evidence. Moderation of your voice, even during argument, suggests control of the situation, both emotionally and intellectually. Your voice alerts the audience to your point of view in two ways:

> **Ethical appeal.** If you project the image of one who knows and cares about the topic, the reader will recognize and respect your deep interest in the subject and the way you have carefully crafted your argument. The reader will also appreciate your attention to research conventions.
>
> **Logical appeal.** For readers to believe in your position, you must provide sufficient evidence in the form of statistical data, paraphrases, and direct quotations from authorities on the subject.

The issue of organ donation, for example, elicits different reactions. Some people argue from the logical position that organs are available and should be used for those in need. Others argue from the ethical position that organs might be harvested prematurely or that organ donation violates religious principles. As a writer, you must balance your ethical and logical appeals to your readers.

Focusing the Final Thesis or Hypothesis

Refining your thesis may keep your paper on track. A thesis expresses a theory that you hope to support with evidence and arguments. A hypothesis is a theory that you hope to prove by investigating, testing, and/or observing. Both the thesis and the hypothesis are propositions that you want to maintain, analyze, and prove. A final thesis or hypothesis performs three tasks:

1. Establishes a claim to control and focus the entire paper.
2. Provides unity and a sense of direction.
3. Specifies to the reader the point of the research.

For example, one student started with the topic "exorbitant tuition," narrowed it to the phrase "tuition fees put parents in debt," and ultimately crafted this thesis:

> The exorbitant tuition at America's colleges is forcing out the poor and promoting an elitist class.

The statement above focuses the argument on the effects of high fees on enrollment. The student needs to prove the assertion by gathering and tabulating statistics.

Questions will focus the thesis. If you have trouble finding a claim or argument, ask yourself a few questions. One of the answers might serve as the thesis or the hypothesis.

- What is the point of my research?

    HYPOTHESIS: A delicate balance of medicine, diet, and exercise can control diabetes mellitus.

- Can I tell the reader anything new or different?

    HYPOTHESIS: Most well water in Rutherford County is unsafe for drinking.

- Do I have a solution to the problem?

    THESIS: Public support for "safe" houses will provide a haven for children who are abused by their parents.

- Do I have a new slant and new approach to the issue?

    HYPOTHESIS: Poverty, not greed, forces many youngsters into a life of crime.

- Should I take the minority view of this matter?

    THESIS: Give credit where it is due: Custer may have lost the battle at Little Bighorn, but Crazy Horse and his men, with inspiration from Sitting Bull, won the battle.

- Will an enthymeme serve my purpose by making a claim in a *because* clause?

    ENTHYMEME: Sufficient organ and tissue donation, enough to satisfy the demand, remains almost impossible because negative myths and religious concerns dominate the minds of many people.

Key words will focus the thesis or the hypothesis. Use the important words from your notes and rough outline to refine your thesis sentence. For example, during your reading of several novels or short stories by Flannery O'Connor, you might have jotted down certain repetitions of image, theme, or character. The key words might be *death, ironic moments of humor, hysteria and passion, human shortcomings,* or other issues that O'Connor repeatedly explored. These concrete ideas might point you toward a general thesis:

> The tragic endings of Flannery O'Connor's stories depict desperate people coming face to face with their own shortcomings.

Change your thesis but not your hypothesis. Be willing to abandon your preliminary thesis if research leads you to new and different issues. However, a hypothesis *cannot* be adjusted or changed. It will be proved true, partially true, or untrue. Your negative findings have value, for you will have disproved the hypothesis so that others need not duplicate your research. For example, the hypothesis might assert: "Industrial pollution is seeping into water tables and traveling many miles into neighboring well water of Lamar County." Your report may prove the truth of the hypothesis, but it may not. It may only establish a probability and the need for additional research.

CHECKLIST: Writing the Final Thesis or Hypothesis

You should be able to answer "yes" to each question below:

☐ Does the thesis express your position in a full, declarative statement that is not a question, not a statement of purpose, and not merely a topic?

☐ Does it limit the subject to a narrow focus that grows out of research?

☐ Does it establish an investigation, interpretation, or theoretical presentation?

☐ Does it point forward to your findings and a discussion of the implications in your conclusion?

9c Writing an Academic Title

A clearly expressed title, like a good thesis statement, focuses your writing and keeps you on course. Although writing a final title may not be feasible until the paper is written, the preliminary title can provide specific words of identification to help you stay focused. For example, one writer began with the title: "Diabetes." Then, to make it more specific, the writer added another word to make "Diabetes Management." As research developed and she recognized the role of medicine, diet, and exercise for victims, she refined the title even more: "Diabetes Management: A Delicate Balance of Medicine, Diet, and Exercise." Thereby, she and her readers had a clear idea that the paper was about three methods of managing the disease.

Long titles are standard in scholarly writing. Consider the following examples:

1. Subject, colon, and focusing phrase:

   Organ and Tissue Donation and Transplantation: Myths, Ethical Issues, and Lives Saved

2. Subject, focusing prepositional phrase:

   Gothic Madness in Three Southern Writers

3. Subject, colon, and type of study:

   Black Dialect in Maya Angelou's Poetry: A Language Study

4. Subject, colon, and focusing question:

   AIDS: Where Did It Come From?

5. Subject, comparative study:

   Religious Imagery in N. Scott Momaday's *The Names* and Heronimous Storm's *Seven Arrows*

9d Drafting the Paper

As you begin drafting your research report, work systematically through your research journal, preliminary plan, or outline to keep order as your notes expand your research (see pages 79–86 for models of organization). Use your notes, photocopies, downloaded material, and research journal to transfer materials directly into the text, remembering always to provide citations to borrowed information. Do not quote an entire paragraph unless it is crucial to your discussion and you cannot easily reduce it to a summary. In addition, be conscious of basic writing conventions, as described next.

Writing with Unity and Coherence

Unity refers to exploring one topic in depth to give your writing a single vision. With unity, each paragraph carefully expands upon a single aspect of the narrowed subject. *Coherence* connects the parts logically by:

- Repetition of key words and sentence structures.
- The judicious use of pronouns and synonyms.

- The effective placement of transitional words and phrases (e.g., *also, furthermore, therefore, in addition,* and *thus*).

The next passage reads with unity (it keeps its focus) and coherence (it repeats key words and uses transitions effectively, as shown in highlighted type).

> Talk shows are spectacles and forms of dramatic entertainment; therefore, members of the studio audience are acting out parts in the drama, like a Greek chorus, just as the host, the guest, and the television viewers are actors as well. Furthermore, some sort of interaction with the "characters" in this made-for-television "drama" happens all the time. If we read a book or attend a play, we question the text, we question the presentation, and we determine for ourselves what it means to us.

Writing in the Proper Tense

Verb tense often distinguishes a paper in the humanities from one in the natural and social sciences. Use the **past tense** in the social sciences and the physical sciences (see pages 111–112). Use the **present tense** in the humanities. MLA style employs the present tense to cite an author's work (e.g., "Patel *explains*" or "the work of Scoggin and Rodriguez *shows*"). The ideas and the words of the writers remain in print and continue to be true in the universal present. Therefore, when writing a paper in the humanities, use the historical present tense, as shown here:

> "It was the best of times, it was the worst of times," writes Charles Dickens about the eighteenth century.

> Johnson argues that sociologist Norman Wayman has a "narrow-minded view of clerics and their role in the community" (64).

Using the Language of the Discipline

Every discipline and every topic has its own vocabulary. Therefore, while reading and taking notes, jot down words and phrases relevant to your research study. Get comfortable with them so you can use them effectively. For example, a child abuse topic requires the language of sociology and psychology, thereby demanding an acquaintance with the following terms:

social worker	maltreatment	aggressive behavior
poverty levels	guardians	hostility
stress	battered child	incestuous relations
formative years	recurrence	behavioral patterns

Many writers create a terminology list to strengthen their command of appropriate nouns and verbs for the subject in question.

Using Source Material to Enhance Your Writing

Readers want to see your thoughts and ideas on a subject. For this reason, a paragraph should seldom contain source material only; it must contain a topic sentence to establish a point for the research evidence. Every paragraph should explain, analyze, and support a thesis, not merely string together a set of quotations. The following passage effectively cites two different sources.

> Two factors that have played a part in farmland becoming drought prone are "light, sandy soil and soils with high alkalinity" (Boughman 234). In response, Bjornson says that drought resistant plants exist along parts of the Mediterranean Sea. Thus, hybrids of these plants may serve Texas farmers (34).

The short passage weaves the sources effectively into a whole, uses the sources as a natural extension of the discussion, and cites each source separately with appropriate citations.

Writing in the Third Person

Write your paper with third-person narration, avoiding phrasing such as "I believe" or "It is my opinion." Rather than writing, "I think television violence affects children," drop the opening two words and write, "Television violence affects children." Readers will understand that the statement is your thought and one that you will defend with evidence.

Writing with the Passive Voice in an Appropriate Manner

The passive voice is often less forceful than an active verb. However, research writers sometimes need to use the passive voice verb, as shown here:

> Forty-three students of a third-grade class at Barksdale School were observed for two weeks.

Use of the passive voice is fairly standard in the social sciences and the natural or applied sciences. The passive voice is preferred because it keeps the focus on the subject of the research, not the writer (you would not want to say, "I observed the students").

Placing Graphics Effectively in a Research Essay

Use graphics to support your text. Most computers allow you to create tables, line graphs, or pie charts as well as diagrams, maps, and other original designs. You may also import tables and illustrations from your sources. Place these graphics as close as possible to the parts of the text to which they relate. It is acceptable to use full-color art if your printer will print in colors; however, use black for the captions and date. Place a full-page graphic design on a separate sheet after making a textual reference to it (e.g., "see Table 7"). Place graphic designs in an appendix when you have several complex items that might distract the reader from your textual message. See page 221 in the Appendix for help with designing tables, line graphs, illustrations, pie charts, and other visuals.

Avoiding Sexist and Biased Language

The best writers exercise caution against words that may stereotype any person, regardless of gender, race, nationality, creed, age, sexual orientation, or disability. The following are some guidelines to help you avoid discriminatory language:

Age. Review the accuracy of your statement of age. It is appropriate to use *boy* and *girl* for children of high school age and under. *Young man* and *young woman* or *male adolescent* and *female adolescent* can be appropriate, but *teenager* carries a certain bias. Avoid *elderly* as a noun; use *older persons.*

Gender. *Gender* is a matter of our culture that identifies men and women within their social groups. *Sex* tends to be a biological factor (see below for a discussion of sexual orientation).

- Use plural subjects so that nonspecific, plural pronouns are grammatically correct. For example, you may specify that Judy Jones maintains *her* lab equipment in sterile condition or indicate that technicians, in general, maintain *their* own equipment.

- Reword the sentence so that a pronoun is unnecessary, as in *The doctor prepared the necessary surgical equipment without interference.*

- Use pronouns that denote gender only when necessary and only when gender has been previously established, as in *Mary, as a new laboratory technician, must learn to maintain her equipment in sterile condition.*

- Use *woman* or *women* in most instances (e.g., *a woman's intuition*), except use *female* for species and statistics, (e.g., *four female subjects*). Avoid the use of *lady,* as in *lady pilot.*

- Use a person's full name (e.g., Ernest Hemingway or Joan Didion) when first mentioned; thereafter use only the surname (e.g., Hemingway or Didion). In general, avoid formal titles (e.g., Dr., Gen., Mrs., Ms., Lt., or Professor) and their equivalents in other languages (e.g., Mme., Dame, or Monsieur).
- Avoid unparallel terms such as *man and wife* or *7 men and 16 females*. Keep terms parallel by saying *husband and wife* or *man and woman* and *7 male rats and 16 female rats*.

Sexual Orientation. The term *sexual orientation* is preferred to the term *sexual preference*. It is preferable to use *lesbians* and *gay men* rather than *homosexuals*. The terms *heterosexual, homosexual,* and *bisexual* can be used to describe both the identity and the behavior of subjects.

Ethnic and Racial Identity. Some persons prefer the term *Black*, others prefer *African American,* and still others prefer *a person of color*. The terms *Negro* and *Afro-American* are dated and inappropriate. Use *Black* and *White,* not the lowercase *black* and *white*. In like manner, some individuals may prefer *Hispanic or Latino*. Use the term *Asian* or *Asian American* rather than *Oriental*. *Native American* is a broad term that includes *Samoans, Hawaiians,* and *American Indians*. A good rule of thumb is to use a person's nationality when it is known (*Mexican, Canadian, Comanche,* or *Nigerian*).

Disability. In general, place people first, not their disability. Rather than *disabled person* or *retarded child* say *person who has scoliosis* or *a child with Down syndrome*. Avoid saying *a challenged person* or *a special child* in favor of *a person with* or *a child with*. Remember that a *disability* is a physical quality, while a *handicap* is a limitation that might be imposed by nonphysical factors, such as poverty or social attitudes.

9e Creating an Introduction, a Body, and a Conclusion

Writing the Introduction

Use the first few paragraphs of your paper to establish the nature of your study.

SUBJECT: Does your introduction identify your specific topic, and then define, limit, and narrow it to one issue?

BACKGROUND: Does your introduction provide relevant historical data or discuss a few key sources that touch on your specific issue?

PROBLEM: Does your introduction identify a problem and explain the complications that your research paper will explore or resolve?

THESIS: Does your introduction use your thesis or hypothesis within the first few paragraphs to establish the direction of the study and to point your readers toward your eventual conclusions?

How you work these essential elements into the beginning of your paper will depend upon your style of writing. They need not appear in this order. Nor should you cram all these items into a short opening paragraph. Feel free to write a long introduction by using more than one of these techniques:

- Open with your thesis or hypothesis.
- Open with a quotation.
- Relate your topic to the well known.
- Provide background information.
- Review the literature.
- Provide a brief summary.
- Define key terms.
- Supply data, statistics, and special evidence.
- Take exception to critical views.
- Use an anecdote as a hook to draw your reader into the essay.

The following sample of an introduction gives background information, establishes a persuasive position, reviews key literature, takes exception, gives key terms, and offers a thesis.

John Berendt's popular and successful novel *Midnight in the Garden of Good and Evil* skillfully presents the unpredictable twists and turns of a landmark murder case set under the moss-hung live oaks of Savannah, Georgia. While it is written as a novel, the nonfiction account of this tragic murder case reveals the intriguing and sometimes deranged relationships that thrive in a town where everyone knows everyone else. However, the mystique of the novel does not lie with the murder case but with the collection of unusual and often complex characters, including a voodoo priestess, a young Southern gigolo, and a Black drag queen (e.g., Bilkin, Miller, and especially Carson, who describes the people of Savannah as "a type of Greek chorus" [14]). Berendt's success lies in his carefully crafted characterization.

Writing the Body of the Research Paper

When writing the body, you should keep in mind three elements:

ANALYSIS: Classify the major issues of the study and provide a careful analysis of each in defense of your thesis.

PRESENTATION: Provide well-reasoned statements at the beginning of your paragraphs and supply evidence of support with proper documentation.

PARAGRAPHS: Offer a variety of development to compare, show process, narrate the history of the subject, and show causes.

Use these techniques to build substantive paragraphs for your paper:

- Relate a time sequence.
- Compare or contrast issues, the views of experts, and nature of literary characters.
- Develop cause and effect.
- Issue a call to action.
- Define key terminology.
- Show a process.
- Ask questions and provide answers.
- Cite evidence from source materials.
- Explain the methods used and the design of the study.
- Present the results of the investigation with data, statistics, and graphics.

The following paragraph demonstrates the use of several techniques—an overview of the problem, citing a source, comparing issues, cause and effect, key terms, and process.

> To burn or not to burn the natural forests in the national parks is the question. The pyrophobia public voices its protest while environmentalists praise the rejuvenating effects of a good forest fire. It is difficult to convince people that not all fire is bad. The public has visions of Smokey Bear campaigns and mental images of Bambi and Thumper fleeing the roaring flames. Chris Bolgiano explains that federal policy evolved slowly "from the basic impulse to douse all fires immediately to a sophisticated decision matrix based on the functions of any given unit of land" (23). Bolgiano declares that "timber production, grazing, recreation, and wilderness preservation elicit different fire-management approaches" (23).

Writing the Conclusion of the Paper

The conclusion is not a summary; it is a discussion of beliefs and findings based on your reasoning and on the evidence and results you have presented. Select appropriate items from this list.

THESIS: Reaffirm the thesis, the hypothesis, or the central mission of your study. If appropriate, give a statement in support or nonsupport of an original enthymeme or hypothesis.

JUDGMENT: Discuss and interpret the findings. Give answers. Now is the time to draw inferences, to emphasize a theory, and to find relevance in the results.

DIRECTIVES: Based on the theoretical implications of the study, offer suggestions for action and for new research.

DISCUSSION: Discuss the implications of your findings from testing or observation.

Use these techniques to write the conclusion:

- Restate the thesis and reach beyond it.
- Close with an effective quotation.
- Return the focus of a literary study to the author.
- Compare the past to the present.
- Offer a directive or a solution.
- Give a call to action.
- Discuss the implications of your findings.

The following example of a conclusion provides an interpretation of the results of an experiment as well as the implications of the results.

The results of this experiment were similar to expectations, but perhaps the statistical significance, because of the small subject size, was biased toward the delayed conditions of the curve. Barker and Peay have addressed this point. The subjects were not truly representative of the total population because of their prior exposure to test procedures. Another factor that may have affected the curves was the presentation of the data. The images on the screen were available for five seconds, and that amount of time may have enabled the subjects to store each image effectively. If the time period for each image were reduced to one or two seconds, there could be lower recall scores, thereby reducing the differences between the control group and the experimental group.

9f Revising the Rough Draft

Once you have the complete paper in a rough draft, the serious business of editing begins. First, you should revise your paper on a global scale, moving blocks of material around so that it is presented logically and in the correct style. Second, edit the draft with a line-by-line examination of wording and technical excellence. Third, proofread the final version to assure that your words are spelled correctly and the text is grammatically sound.

Revision can turn a passable paper into an excellent one. Revise the manuscript on a global scale by looking at its overall design. Do the introduction, body, and conclusion have substance? Do the paragraphs maintain the flow of your central proposition? Does the paper fulfill the requirements of the academic model?

Editing before Printing the Final Manuscript

Global revision is complemented by careful editing of paragraphs, sentences, and individual words. Travel through the paper to study your citation of the sources. Confirm that you have properly cited each quoted or paraphrased source. Use your spell-checker and then re-read your paper, looking for misspellings. Here are eight additional tasks:

1. Cut phrases and sentences that do not advance your main ideas or that merely repeat what your sources have already stated.
2. Determine that coordinated, balanced ideas are appropriately expressed and that minor ideas are properly subordinated.
3. Change most of your "to be" verbs (is, are, was) to stronger active verbs.
4. Maintain the present tense of most verbs.
5. Convert passive structures to active unless you want to emphasize the subject, not the actor (see page 119).
6. Confirm that you have introduced paraphrases and quotations so that they flow smoothly in your text.
7. Use formal, academic style and be on guard against clusters of little monosyllabic words that fail to advance ideas. Examine your wording for its effectiveness within the context of your subject (see pages 117–119).
8. Examine your paragraphs for effective transitions that move the reader from one paragraph to the next.

Using the Computer to Edit Your Text

Some software programs will examine your grammar and mechanics, look for parentheses that you opened but never closed, find unpaired quotation marks, flag passive verbs, question your spelling, and mark other items for your correction. Pay attention to the caution flags raised by this type of program. After a software program examines the style of your manuscript, you should revise and edit the text to improve stylistic weaknesses. Remember, it is your paper, not the computer's document, so use your knowledge of grammar and writing mechanics when making revisions.

Participating in Peer Review

Peer review has two sides. First, it means handing your paper to a friend or classmate, asking for their opinions and suggestions. Second, it means reviewing a classmate's research paper. You can learn by reviewing as well as by writing. Your instructor may supply a peer review sheet, or you can use the accompanying checklist. Criticize the paper constructively on each point.

CHECKLIST: Peer Review

1. Are the subject and the accompanying issues introduced early?
2. Is the writer's critical approach to the problem stated clearly in a thesis sentence? Is it placed effectively in the introduction?
3. Do the paragraphs of the body have individual unity? That is, does each one develop an important idea and only one idea? Does each paragraph relate to the thesis?
4. Are sources introduced, usually with the name of the expert, and then cited by a page number within parentheses? Keep in mind that Internet sources will not have page numbers.
5. Is it clear where a paraphrase begins and where it ends?
6. Are the sources relevant to the argument?
7. Does the writer weave quotations into the text effectively while avoiding long quotations that look like filler instead of substance?
8. Does the conclusion arrive at a resolution about the central issue?
9. Does the title describe clearly what your classmate has put in the body of the paper?

Proofreading

Print a hard copy of your manuscript. Proofread this final version with great care before submitting it to your instructor.

CHECKLIST: Proofreading

1. Check for errors in sentence structure, spelling, and punctuation.
2. Check for hyphenation and word division. Try to avoid hyphenating words at the ends of lines.
3. Read each quotation to ensure that your own wording and the words within your quoted materials are accurate. Check for opening and closing quotation marks.
4. Double-check in-text citations to be certain that each one is correct and that each source is listed on your Works Cited page at the end of the paper.
5. Double-check the format—the title page, margins, spacing, content notes, and other elements.

Blending Reference Material into Your Writing by Using MLA Style

Your in-text citations should conform to standards announced by your instructor. This chapter explains the MLA style, as established by the Modern Language Association. It governs papers in freshman composition, literature, English usage, and foreign languages.

The MLA style puts great emphasis on the writer of the source, asking for the full name of the scholar on first mention but last name only thereafter and last name only in parenthetical citations. Other styles emphasize the year of publication as well as the author. Still other styles use merely a number in order to emphasize the material, not the author or date.

10a Blending Reference Citations into Your Text

As you might expect, writing a research paper carries with it certain obligations. You should gather scholarly material on the topic and display it prominently in your writing. In addition, you should identify each source used with the author's name or the title of the work with a page number, except for unprinted sources and most Internet sources, which will not require a page number. As a general policy, keep citations brief. Remember, your readers will have full documentation to each source on the Works Cited page (see Chapter 11).

Making a General Reference without a Page Number

Sometimes you will need no parenthetical citation.

> The women of Thomas Hardy's novels are the special focus of three essays by Nancy Norris, Judith Mitchell, and James Scott.

Beginning with the Author and Ending with a Page Number

Introduce a quotation or a paraphrase with the author's name and close it with a page number, placed inside the parentheses. Try always to use this standard citation format because it informs the reader of the beginning and the end of borrowed materials, as shown here:

> Herbert Norfleet states that the use of video games by children improves their hand and eye coordination (45).

In the following example, the reader can easily trace the origin of the ideas.

> Video games for children have opponents and advocates. Herbert Norfleet defends the use of video games by children. He says it improves their hand and eye coordination and that it exercises their minds as they work their way through various puzzles and barriers. Norfleet states, "The mental gymnastics of video games and the competition with fellow players are important to young children for their physical, social, and mental development" (45). Yet some authorities disagree with Norfleet for several reasons.

Putting the Page Number Immediately after the Name

Sometimes, notes at the end of a quotation make it expeditious to place the page number immediately after the name.

> Boughman (46) urges car makers to "direct the force of automotive airbags *upward* against the windshield" (emphasis added).

Putting the Name and Page Number at the End of Borrowed Material

You can, if you like, put cited names with the page number at the end of a quotation or paraphrase.

> "Each DNA strand provides the pattern of bases for a new strand to form, resulting in two complete molecules" (Justice, Moody, and Graves 462).

In the case of a paraphrase, you should give your reader a signal to show when the borrowing begins, as shown next:

> One source explains that the DNA in the chromosomes must be copied perfectly during cell reproduction (Justice, Moody, and Graves 462).

Use last names only within the parenthetical citation *unless your list contains more than one author with the same last name,* in which case you should add the author's first initial—for example, (H. Norfleet 45) and (W. Norfleet 432). If the first initial is also shared, use the full first name: (Herbert Norfleet 45).

HINT

In MLA style, do not place a comma between the name and the page number.

10b Citing a Source When No Author Is Listed

When no author is shown on a title page, cite the title of the article, the name of the magazine, the name of a bulletin or book, or the name of the publishing organization. You should abbreviate or use an acronym for such sources (e.g., BBC, NASA).

HINT

Search for the author's name at the bottom of the opening page, at the end of the article, at an Internet home page, or in an e-mail address.

Citing the Title of a Magazine Article

Use a shorted version of the title when no author is listed:

> The impending separation of Northern and Southern states which led
> to the American Civil War was most clearly realized as the nation prepared for
> the presidential election of 1860. According to a recent article in ⃞America's
> Civil War magazine,⃞ nine states in the South "firmly refused to include
> Republican candidate Abraham Lincoln on the ballot" ⃞("Open Fire").⃞

The Works Cited entry would read:

> "Open Fire!" *America's Civil War.* May 2008: 12. Print.

Citing the Title of a Report

> One bank showed a significant decline in assets despite an increase in
> its number of depositors ⃞(*Annual Report,*⃞ 2008, 23).

Citing the Name of a Publisher or a Corporate Body

> The report by the ⃞Clarion County School Board⃞ endorsed the use
> of Channel One in the school system and said that "students will benefit by
> the news reports more than they will be adversely affected by advertising"
> (CCSB 3–4).

10c Citing Nonprint Sources That Have No Page Number

On occasion you may need to identify nonprint sources, such as a
speech, the song lyrics from a CD, an interview, or a television program. Since no page number exists, omit the parenthetical citation.
Instead, introduce the type of source—for example, lecture, letter,
interview—so readers do not expect a page number.

> ⃞Thompson's lecture⃞ defined *impulse* as "an action triggered by the
> nerves without thought for the consequences."

> Mrs. Peggy Meacham said ⃞in her phone interview⃞ that prejudice against
> young Black women is not as severe as that against young Black males.

10d Citing Internet Sources

Identify the Source with Name or Title

Whenever possible, identify the author of an Internet article. Usually, no page number is listed.

> Hershel Winthrop interprets Hawthorne's stories as the search for holiness in a corrupt Puritan society.

If you can't identify an author, give the article title or Web site information.

> One Web site claims that any diet that avoids carbohydrates will avoid some sugars that are essential for the body ("Fad Diets").

Identify the Nature of the Information and Its Credibility

As a service to your reader, indicate your best estimate of the scholarly value of an Internet source. For example, the next citation explains the role of the Center for Communication Policy:

> The UCLA Center for Communication Policy, which conducted an intensive study of television violence, has advised against making the television industry the "scapegoat for violence" by advocating a focus on "deadlier and more significant causes: inadequate parenting, drugs, underclass rage, unemployment and availability of weaponry."

Here's another example of an introduction that establishes credibility:

> John Armstrong, a spokesperson for Public Electronic Access to Knowledge (PEAK), states:
>
> As we venture into this age of biotechnology, many people predict gene manipulation will be a powerful tool for improving the quality of life. They foresee plants engineered to resist pests, animals designed to produce large quantities of rare medicinals, and humans treated by gene therapy to relieve suffering.

Note: To learn more about the source of an Internet article, as in the case immediately above, learn to search out a home page. The address for Armstrong's article is **http://www.ifgene.org/overview.htm**. By truncating the address to **http://www.ifgene.org/** you can learn about the organization that Armstrong represents.

If you are not certain about the credibility of a source—that is, it seemingly has no scholarly or educational basis—do not cite it, or describe the source so readers can make their own judgments:

> An Iowa nonprofit organization, the Mothers for Natural Law, says— but offers no proof —that eight major crops are affected by genetically engineered organisms—canola, corn, cotton, dairy products, potatoes, soybeans, tomatoes, and yellow crook-neck squash ("What's on the Market").

Omitting Page and Paragraph Numbers to Internet Citations

In general, you should not list a page number, paragraph number, or screen number to an Internet site.

- You cannot list a screen number because monitors differ.
- You cannot list a page number of a downloaded document because computer printers differ.
- Unless they are numbered in the document, you cannot list paragraph numbers. Besides, you would have to go through and count every paragraph.

The marvelous feature of electronic text is that it is searchable, so your readers can find your quotation quickly with the Find or Search features. Suppose you have written the following:

> The Television Violence Report advises against making the television industry the "scapegoat for violence" by advocating a focus on "deadlier and more significant causes: inadequate parenting, drugs, underclass rage, unemployment and availability of weaponry."

A reader who wants to investigate further can consult your Works Cited page, find the Internet address (URL), use a browser to locate the article, and use Find for a phrase, such as "scapegoat for violence." That's much easier on you than numbering all the paragraphs and easier on the reader than counting them.

Some academic societies are urging scholars who publish on the Internet to number their paragraphs, and that practice may catch on quickly. Therefore, you should provide a paragraph number if the author of the Internet article has numbered each paragraph.

> The Insurance Institute for Highway Safety emphasizes restraint first, saying, "Riding unrestrained or improperly restrained in a motor vehicle always has been the greatest hazard for children" (par. 13).

XL
SHAKESPEARE'S CONCEPTION OF *HAMLET*

What was Shakespeare's conception of *Hamlet*? That is the question. It is one which inevitably resolves itself into a reconstruction of the materials at his disposal, the dramatic problems with which he had to deal, and the means whereby he sought to satisfy contemporary dramatic taste. For such a reconstruction modern scholarship provides abundant information about both the theatrical practices and intellectual interests of the time and Shakespeare's habits as a craftsman. In particular should be noted his exceptional preoccupation with character portrayal and the scrupulous motivation of action; his conformity with changing theatrical fashion, yet at the same time his reluctance to pioneer in experiment; his sensitive, if sketchy, acquaintance with matters of contemporary interest; and his success as a skilled and inspired adapter rather than as an innovator. In the application of this knowledge two principles are fundamental. First, *Hamlet* must not be viewed as isolation, but in close conjunction with the theatrical environment which produced it. Second, Shakespeare must be recognized as primarily a practical playwright, a business man of the theater with obligations to fulfill, specific theatrical conditions to meet, and an audience to divert. For the rest, it is a pleasant exercise for the recreative imagination to try to think oneself into Shakespeare's mind, to face the problem of *Hamlet* as he faced it, and to trace the solution as he must have found it.

I

Shakespeare's *Hamlet* is a philosophical melodrama. Theatrically it is one of his most spectacular plays. For all its discursiveness it is crammed with action of the most sensational sort. Ghosts walk and cry "Revenge!" Murder is foully done. Conspirators plot and counterplot. Two characters go mad. A queen is terrified nearly to death. A play breaks up in a near-riot. An insurrection batters the palace gates. A brawl desecrates a suicide's grave. A duel explodes into murder and general butchery. There are poison, incest, war, and debauchery. This is not closet drama for the philosopher's study; it is blood and thunder for the popular stage.

Nevertheless, *Hamlet* is also one of Shakespeare's most thoughtful plays. Permeated with moralizing and philosophical speculation, it presents in its center character a most elaborate psychological study. As for the reader these are unquestionably the most enduring elements, so to the elucidation of these criticism has devoted most of its attention.

777

---

778   *Shakespeare's Conception of "Hamlet"*

Indeed, not infrequently is it implied that the play exists for the express purpose of expounding Shakespeare's views on life and death, or that the play is primarily a peg upon which to hang the character of Hamlet. Such a view, however, scarcely squares with the known practice of Shakespeare, or, for that matter, of any successful playwright. The one play of the period which openly advertised itself as a philosophical character study–Chapman's *Revenge of Bussy D'Ambois*–was an inglorious failure. Contrast with this the extraordinary popularity of *Hamlet*, and one may see how much of it depends upon the scrupulous subordination of those very philosophical elements which make Chapman's play so insufferably dull to the modern reader. To Shakespeare, doubtless, both character study and philosophical speculation were distinctly subsidiary to plot and stage business; and in the excised version, which must have been necessary for stage presentation, they probably interfered little with the more congenial business of swift melodrama.[1]

You may cite these page numbers because JSTOR photocopies the original publications.

Harold R. Walley   779

session with a few restricted preoccupations. The peculiarity of Hamlet's madness is that, no matter how insane his ravings may seem to his hearers, without exception they contain *double entendre* and make perfect sense from Hamlet's point of view. The method is substantially that which underlies the contemporaneous intellectual conceit; namely, the surprise association of apparently incongruous elements linked by a submerged chain of thought. Thus whatever madness Hamlet exhibits is an integral part of his own mental attitude.

This mental obsession, which issues in the evidences of Hamlet's supposed madness, is intimately connected with two other important features of the play. Hamlet is much concerned with his inability to carry forward his revenge. This delay is essential to the plot; that it is a delay for which Hamlet is himself responsible Shakespeare makes clear throughout.[2] Much, however, as Hamlet endeavors to understand the reason, he is incapable of explaining it to himself; it is an ingrained part

FIGURE 10.1
You may cite these page numbers.

Provide a page number only if you find original page numbers buried within the electronic article. For example, a database like JSTOR reproduces original images of works and thereby provides original page numbers, as with the article by Harold R. Walley shown in Figure 10.1. Cite these pages just as you would a printed source.

> One source says the "moralizing and philosophical speculation" in *Hamlet* is worthy of examination, but to Shakespeare these were "distinctly subsidiary to plot and stage business . . ." (Walley 778).

CHECKLIST: Using Links to Document Internet Sources

If you are publishing your project on your own Web page, you have the opportunity to send your readers to other sites via hypertext links. If you do so, follow these guidelines:

1. You may activate a hot key (hypertext link) in your document that will automatically send your reader to one of your sources.

2. Identify the linked source clearly so readers know where the link will take them.

3. Be selective; don't sprinkle your document with excessive links. You want the reader to stay with you, not wander around on the Internet.

4. The links are part of your documentation, so cite these linked sources in your Works Cited list.

10e Citing Indirect Sources

Sometimes the writer of a book or article quotes another person from an interview or personal correspondence, and you may want to use that same quotation. For example, in a newspaper article in *USA Today*, page 9A, Karen S. Peterson writes this passage in which she quotes two people:

> Sexuality, popularity, and athletic competition will create anxiety for junior high kids and high schoolers. Eileen Shiff says, "Bring up the topics. Don't wait for them to do it; they are nervous and they want to appear cool." Monitor the amount of time high schoolers spend working for money, she suggests. "Work is important, but school must be the priority." Parental intervention in a child's school career that worked in junior high may not work in high school, psychiatrist Martin Greenburg adds. "The interventions can be construed by the adolescent as negative, overburdening and interfering with the child's ability to care for himself." He adds, "Be encouraging, not critical. Criticism can be devastating for the teenager."

Suppose you want to use the quotation above by Martin Greenburg. You must quote the words of Greenburg *and* put Peterson's name in the parenthetical citation as the person who wrote the article, as shown in the following:

> After students get beyond middle school, they begin to resent interference by their parents, especially in school activities. They need some space from Mom and Dad. Martin Greenburg says, "The interventions can be construed by the adolescent as negative, overburdening and interfering with the child's ability to care for himself" (qtd. in Peterson 9A).

On the Works Cited page, you will list Peterson's name with the bibliography entry for her article, but you will not list Greenburg's name there because he is not the author of the article.

In other words, in the text you need a double reference that introduces the speaker and includes a clear reference to the book or article where you found the quotation or the paraphrased material. Without the reference to Peterson, nobody could find the article. Without the reference to Greenburg, readers would assume Peterson spoke the words.

HINT

If you can locate the original source of the quotation, cite it rather than use the double reference.

10f Citing Frequent Page References to the Same Work

If you quote more than once from the same page within a paragraph and no other citations intervene, you may provide one citation at the end for all the references.

> When the character Beneatha denies the existence of God in Hansberry's *A Raisin in the Sun,* Mama slaps her in the face and forces her to repeat after her, "In my mother's house there is still God." Then Mama adds, "There are some ideas we ain't going to have in this house. Not long as I am at the head of the family" (37).

Also, when you make frequent references to the same source, you need not repeat the author's name in every instance. Note the following example:

> The consumption of "healing foods," such as those that reduce blood pressure, grows in popularity each year. Clare Hasler says that when the medicinal properties of functional food gain the support of clinical evidence, functional foods can become an economical weapon in the battle against rising health care costs. In addition, functional foods may be a promising addition to the diet of people who suffer from deadly disease. As executive director of the Functional Foods for Health Program at the University of Illinois, she claims, "Six of the ten leading causes of death in the United State are believed to be related to diet: cancer, coronary heart disease, stroke, diabetes, atherosclerosis, and liver disease" ("Western Perspective" 66).

HINT

If you are citing from two or more novels in your paper—let's say John Steinbeck's *East of Eden* and *Of Mice and Men*—provide both title (abbreviated) and page(s) unless the reference is clear: (*Eden* 56) and (*Mice* 12–13).

10g Citing Material from Textbooks and Large Anthologies

Reproduced below is a poem that you might find in many literary textbooks.

The Red Wheelbarrow
so much depends
upon
a red wheel
barrow
glazed with rain
water
beside the white chickens

William Carlos Williams

If you quote lines of the poem, and if that is all you quote from the anthology, cite the author and page in the text and put a comprehensive entry in the Works Cited list.

Text:

For Williams, "so much depends" on the red wheel barrow as it sits "glazed with rain water beside the white chickens" (477).

Works Cited entry:

Williams, William Carlos. "The Red Wheelbarrow." *The Literary Experience.* Compact ed. Ed. Bruce Beiderwell and Jeffrey M. Wheeler. Boston: Thomson, Wadsworth, 2008. 477. Print.

Suppose, however, that you also take quotations from other poems in the textbook.

In "Stopping by Woods on a Snowy Evening," Robert Frost looks for an escape into the desolate solitude of the snowy woods, saying "The woods are lovely, dark, and deep" but realizes that his commitments outweigh his personal ambitions, "But I have promises to keep / And miles to go before I sleep" (61).

T. S. Eliot describes the fog as a "yellow smoke" that "Slipped by the terrace, made a sudden leap" (499).

Now, with three citations to the same anthology, you should list in your Works Cited the anthology used, as edited by Beiderwell and Wheeler, and also use shortened citations for Williams, Frost, and Eliot, with each referring to the lead editor's name, in this case *Bruce Beiderwell*.

> Beiderwell, Bruce, and Jeffrey M. Wheeler, eds. *The Literary Experience.* Compact Edition. Boston: Thomson, Wadsworth, 2008. Print.
>
> Eliot, T. S. "The Love Song of J. Alfred Prufrock." Beiderwell. 499–503. Print.
>
> Frost, Robert. "Stopping by Woods on a Snowy Evening." Beiderwell. 61. Print.
>
> Williams, William Carlos. "The Red Wheelbarrow." Beiderwell. 477. Print.

10h Adding Extra Information to In-text Citations

As a courtesy to your reader, add extra information within the citation. Show parts of books, different titles by the same writer, or several works by different writers. For example, your reader may have a different anthology than yours, so a clear reference, such as (*Great Expectations* 81; chap. 4), will enable the reader to locate the passage. The same is true with a reference to (*Romeo and Juliet* 2.3.65–68). The reader will find the passage in almost any edition of Shakespeare's plays. Here's a reference to Herman Melville's *Moby-Dick* that shows both page and chapter:

> Melville uncovers the superstitious nature of Ishmael by stressing Ishmael's fascination with Yojo, the little totem god of Queequeg (71; chap. 16).

One of Several Volumes

These next two citations provide three vital facts: (1) an abbreviation for the title, (2) the volume used, and (3) the page number(s). The Works Cited entry will list the total number of volumes (see pages 173–174).

> In a letter to his Tennessee Volunteers in 1812, General Jackson chastised the "mutinous and disorderly conduct" of some of his troops (*Papers* 2: 348–49).

Joseph Campbell suggests that man is a slave yet also the master of all the gods (*Masks* 2: 472).

However, if you use only one volume of a multivolume work, you need to give only page numbers in the parenthetical reference. Then include the volume number in the Works Cited entry (see page 174):

Don Quixote's strange adventure with the Knight of the Mirrors is one of Cervantes's brilliant short tales (1,908–14).

If you refer to an entire volume, there is no need for page numbers:

The Norton Anthology includes masterpieces of the ancient world, the Middle Ages, and the Renaissance (Mack et al., vol. 1).

Two or More Works by the Same Writer

In this example, the writer makes reference to two novels, both abbreviated. The full titles are *Tess of the D'Urbervilles* and *The Mayor of Casterbridge.*

Thomas Hardy reminds readers in his prefaces that "a novel is an impression, not an argument" and that a novel should be read as "a study of man's deeds and character" (*Tess* xxii; *Mayor* 1).

If the author appears in the parenthetical citation, place a comma after the name: (Hardy, *Tess* xxii; Hardy, *Mayor* 1). If anything other than a page number appears after the title, follow the title with a comma: (Worth, "Computing," par. 6).

The complete titles of the two works by Campbell referenced in the following example are *The Hero with a Thousand Faces* and *The Masks of God,* a four-volume work.

Because he stresses the nobility of man, Joseph Campbell suggests that the mythic hero is symbolic of the "divine creative and redemptive image which is hidden within us all . . ." (*Hero* 39). The hero elevates the human mind to an "ultimate mythogenetic zone—the creator and destroyer, the slave and yet the master, of all the gods" (*Masks* 1: 472).

Several Authors in One Citation

You may wish to cite several sources that treat the same topic. Put them in alphabetical order to match that of the Works Cited page, or place them in the order of importance to the issue at hand. Separate them with semicolons.

> Several sources have addressed this aspect of gang warfare as a fight for survival, not just for control of the local neighborhood or "turf" (Robertson 98–134; Rollins 34; Templass 561–65).

Additional Information with the Page Number

Your citations can refer to special parts of a page—for example, footnote, appendix, graph, table—and can also specify emphasis on particular pages.

> Horton (22, n. 3) suggests that Melville forced the symbolism, but Welston (199–248, esp. 234) reaches an opposite conclusion.

However, use a semicolon to separate the page number from the edition used, a chapter number, or other identifying information: (Wollstonecraft 185; ch. 13, sec. 2).

10i Punctuating Citations Properly and Consistently

Keep page citations outside quotation marks but inside the final period, as shown here:

> "The benefits of cloning far exceed any harm that might occur" (Smith 34).

In MLA style, use no comma between the name and the page within the citation (for example, Jones 16–17, *not* Jones, 16–17). Do not use *p.* or *pp.* with the page number(s) in MLA style. However, if an author's name begins a citation to paragraph numbers or screen numbers, *do* include a comma after the author's name (Richards, par. 4) or (Thompson, screens 6–7).

Commas and Periods

Place commas and periods inside quotation marks unless the page citation intervenes. The example below shows: (1) how to put the mark inside the quotation marks, (2) how to interrupt a quotation to insert the speaker, (3) how to use single quotation marks within the regular quotation marks, and (4) how to place the period after a page citation.

"Modern advertising," says Rachel Murphy, "not only creates a marketplace, it determines values." She adds, "I resist the advertiser's argument that they awaken, not create desires'" (192).

Sometimes you may need to change the closing period to a comma. Suppose you decide to quote this sentence: "Scientific cloning poses no threat to the human species." If you start your sentence with the quotation, you will need to change the period to a comma, as shown:

> "Scientific cloning poses no threat to the human species," declares Joseph Wineberg in a recent article (357).

However, retain question marks or exclamation marks; no comma is required:

> "Does scientific cloning pose a threat to the human species?" wonders Mark Durham (546).

Let's look at other examples. Suppose this is the original material:

> The Russians had obviously anticipated neither the quick discovery of the bases nor the quick imposition of the quarantine. Their diplomats across the world were displaying all the symptoms of improvisation, as if they had been told nothing of the placement of the missiles and had received no instructions what to say about them.—From: Arthur M. Schlesinger, Jr., *A Thousand Days* (New York: Houghton, 1965), 820.

Punctuate citations from this source in one of the following methods in accordance with MLA style:

> "The Russians," writes Schlesinger, "had obviously anticipated neither the quick discovery of the [missile] bases nor the quick imposition of the quarantine" (820).

> Schlesinger notes, "Their diplomats across the world were displaying all the symptoms of improvisation . . ." (820).

> Schlesinger observes that the Russian failure to anticipate an American discovery of Cuban missiles caused "their diplomats across the world" to improvise answers as "if they had been told nothing of the placement of the missiles . . ." (820).

Note that the last example correctly changes the capital *T* of "their" to lower case to match the grammar of the restructured sentence, and it does not use ellipsis points before "if" because the phrase flows smoothly into the text.

Semicolons and Colons

Both semicolons and colons go outside the quotation marks, as illustrated by these three examples:

> Zigler admits that "the extended family is now rare in contemporary society"; however, he stresses the greatest loss as the "wisdom and daily support of older, more experienced family members" (42).

> Zigler laments the demise of the "extended family": that is, the family suffers by loss of the "wisdom and daily support of older, more experienced family members" (42).

> Brian Sutton-Smith says, "Adults don't worry whether *their* toys are educational" (64); nevertheless, parents want to keep their children in a learning mode.

The third example, immediately above, shows how to place the page citation after a quotation and before a semicolon.

Use the semicolon to separate two or more works in a single parenthetical reference:

> (Roman, *Dallas* 16; Manfred 345)
> (Steinbeck, *Grapes* 24; Stuben xii)

Question Marks and Exclamation Marks

When a question mark or an exclamation mark serves as part of the quotation, keep it inside the quotation mark. Put the page citation immediately after the name of the source to avoid conflict with the punctuation mark.

> Thompson (16) passionately shouted to union members, "We can bring order into our lives even though we face hostility from every quarter!"

If you place the page number at the end of the quotation, retain the original exclamation mark or question mark, follow with the page reference, and then a sentence period outside the citation.

> Thompson passionately shouted to union members, "We can bring order into our lives even though we face hostility from every quarter!" (16).

Retain question marks and exclamation marks when the quotation begins a sentence; no comma is required.

> "We face hostility from every quarter!" declared the union leader.

Question marks appear inside the closing quotation mark when they are part of the original quotation; otherwise, they go outside.

> The philosopher Brackenridge (16) asks, "How should we order our lives?"

and

> The philosopher Brackenridge asks, "How should we order our lives?" (16).

but

> Did Brackenridge say that we might encounter "hostility from every quarter" (16)?

Single Quotation Marks

When a quotation appears within another quotation, use single quotation marks with the shorter one. The period goes inside both closing quotation marks.

> George Loffler (32) confirms that "the unconscious carries the best of human thought and gives man great dignity, but it also has the dark side so that we cry, in the words of Shakespeare's Macbeth, 'Hence, horrible shadow! Unreal mockery, hence.'"

Remember that the period always goes inside quotation marks unless the page citation intervenes, as shown below:

> George Loffler confirms that "the unconscious carries the best of human thought and gives man great dignity, but it also has the dark side so that we cry, in the words of Shakespeare's Macbeth, 'Hence, horrible shadow! Unreal mockery, hence'" (32).

10j Indenting Long Quotations

Set off long prose quotations of four lines or more by indenting 1 inch or 10 spaces, which is usually two clicks of the tab key. Do not enclose the indented material within quotation marks. If you quote only one paragraph or the beginning of one, do *not* indent the first line an extra five spaces. Maintain normal double-spacing between your text and the quoted materials. Place the parenthetical citation *after* the final mark of punctuation. As shown below, the parenthetical citation might be a title to an Internet article rather than to page numbers:

> The number of people who need transplants continues to increase, but the number of donors fails to meet these needs. Tommy G. Thompson, secretary for the Department of Health and Human Services, commented on the current state of organ donation:
>
>> Citing the growing need for organ donation to save and improve lives, Tommy G. Thompson, within his first 100 days as HHS Secretary, announced his commitment to develop a new national effort to encourage organ donation. That commitment, also known as the Gift of Life Donation Initiative, led to 2007's record transplant totals through which the number of transplant candidates who died waiting for an organ fell below 6,000 for the first time in six years. ("New Record")
>
> With the ever-increasing number of organ donors needed, why don't people give of themselves? The most recognized reason for the shortage of donors is directly related to the myths that are associated with organ and tissue donation.

If you quote more than one paragraph, indent all paragraphs an extra three spaces or a quarter-inch. However, if the first sentence quoted does not begin a paragraph in the original source, do not indent it an extra three spaces.

> Zigler makes this observation:
> With many others, I am nevertheless optimistic that our nation will eventually display its inherent greatness and successfully correct the many ills that I have touched upon here.
>
>> Of course, much remains that could and should be done, including increased efforts in the area of family planning, the widespread implementation of Education for Parenthood programs, an increase in the availability of homemaker and child care services, and a reexamination of our commitment to doing what is in the best interest of every child in America. (42)

10k Citing Poetry

Quoting Two Lines of Poetry or Less

Incorporate short quotations of poetry (one or two lines) into your text.

> In Part 3, Eliot's "The Waste Land" (1922) remains a springtime search for nourishing water: "Sweet Thames, run softly, for I speak not loud or long"

(line 12) says the speaker in "The Fire Sermon," while in Part 5 the speaker of "What the Thunder Said" yearns for "a damp gust / Bringing rain" (73–74).

As the example demonstrates:

1. Set off the material with quotation marks.
2. Indicate separate lines by using a virgule (/) with a space before and after it.
3. Place line documentation within parentheses immediately following the quotation mark and inside the period. Do not use the abbreviations *l.* or *ll.*, which might be confused with page numbers; use *lines* initially to establish that the numbers represent lines of poetry, and thereafter use only the numbers.
4. Use Arabic numerals for books, parts, volumes, and chapters of works; acts, scenes, and lines of plays; and cantos, stanzas, and lines of poetry.

Quoting Three Lines of Poetry or More

Set off three or more lines of poetry by indenting 1 inch or 10 spaces, as shown below. Use double-spaced lines. A parenthetical citation to the lines of indented verse follows the last line of the quotation. If the parenthetical citation will not fit on the last line, place it on the next line, flush with the right margin of the poetry text.

> The king cautions Prince Henry:
>> Thy place in council thou has rudely lost,
>> Which by thy younger brother is supplied,
>> And art almost an alien to the hearts
>> Of all the court and princes of my blood.
>
> (3.2.32–35)

Refer to act, scene, and lines only after you have established Shakespeare's *Henry IV*, Part 1 as the central topic of your study; otherwise, write (IH4 3.2.32–35). If you are citing from more than one play, always add an abbreviation for the play (1H4 1.1.15–18).

Indenting Turnovers for Long Lines of Poetry

When quoting a line of poetry that is too long for your right margin, indent the continuation line three spaces or a quarter-inch more than the greatest indentation.

Plath opens her poem with these lines:

> Love set you going like a fat gold watch.
> The midwife slapped your footsoles,
> and your bald cry
> Took its place among the elements. (lines 1–3)

You may also indent less to make room for the words:

Plath opens her poem with these lines:

> Love set you going like a fat gold watch.
> The midwife slapped your footsoles, and your bald cry
> Took its place among the elements. (lines 1–3)

NOTE

For using ellipsis points with poetry, see page 148.

Retaining Internal Quotations within a Block

While you should not use quotation marks around a block quotation, *do* retain any internal quotation marks:

With his sonnet "Spring," Shakespeare playfully describes the cry of the cuckoo bird:

> The cuckoo then, on every tree,
> Mocks married men; for thus sings he, "Cuckoo!
> Cuckoo, cuckoo!" O word of fear,
> Unpleasing to a married ear! (524)

Providing Translations

When a quotation is run into the text, use double quotation marks for translations placed within parentheses but single quotations around a translation without the parentheses:

Chaucer's setting is Spring, when "zephyrs ("west winds") have breathed softly all about . . ." (line 5).

Chaucer's setting is Spring, when "zephyrs 'west winds' have breathed softly all about . . ." (line 5).

Do not place quotation marks around quotations and translations set off from the text in a block. Place the block of translation below the block of poetry.

Ramon Magrans has translated this Lorca poem in a literal manner:

> Alto pinar!

Cuatro palomas por el aire van.

Cuatro palomas

Vuelan y tornan

Llevan heridas

sus cuatro sombras

Bajo pinar!

Cuatro palomas en la tierra están.

Above the pine trees

four pigeons fly through the air.

Four pigeons

fly and turn around

Wounded, they carry

their four shadows.

Below the pine trees

four pigeons lie on the earth.

10l Handling Quotations from a Play

Set off from your text any dialog of two or more characters. Begin with the character's name, indented one inch and written in all capital letters. Follow the name with a period, and then start the character's lines of dialog. Indent subsequent lines of dialog an additional quarter-inch or three spaces.

At the end of *Oedipus Rex,* Kreon chastises Oedipus, reminding him that he no longer has control over his own life nor that of his children.

> KREON.   Come now and leave your children.
> OEDIPUS.   No! Do not take them from me!
> KREON.   Think no longer
>   That you are in command here,
>   but rather think
>   How, when you were, you served
>   your own destruction.

10m Altering Initial Capitals in Quoted Matter

In general, you should reproduce quoted materials exactly, yet one exception is permitted for logical reasons. Restrictive connectors, such as *that* and *because*, create restrictive clauses and eliminate a need for the comma. Without a comma, the capital letter is unnecessary. In the following example, "The," which is capitalized as the first word in the original sentence, is changed to lowercase because it continues the grammatical flow of the student's sentence.

> Another writer argues that "the single greatest impediment to our improving the lives of America's children is the myth that we are a child-oriented society" (Zigler 39).

Otherwise, write:

> Another writer argues, "The single greatest. . . ."

10n Omitting Quoted Matter with Ellipsis Points

You may omit portions of quoted material with three spaced ellipsis points, as shown in the following examples.

Context

In omitting passages, be fair to the author. Do not change the meaning or take a quotation out of context.

Correctness

Maintain the grammatical correctness of your sentences—that is, avoid fragments and misplaced modifiers. You don't want your readers to misunderstand the structure of the original. When you quote only a phrase, readers will understand that you omitted most of the original sentence, so no ellipsis is necessary.

> Phil Withim recognizes the weakness in Captain Vere's "intelligence and insight" into the significance of his decisions regarding Billy Budd (118).

Omission within a Sentence

Use three ellipsis points (periods) with a space before each and a space after the last.

> Phil Withim objects to the idea that "such episodes are intended to demonstrate that Vere . . . has the intelligence and insight to perceive the deeper issue" (118).

Omission at the End of a Sentence

If an ellipsis occurs at the end of your sentence, use three periods with a space before each following a sentence period—that is, you will have four periods with no space before the first or after the last. A closing quotation mark finishes the punctuation.

> R. W. B. Lewis (62) declares that "if Hester has sinned, she has done so as an affirmation of life, and her sin is the source of life . . ."

However, if a page citation also appears at the end in conjunction with the ellipsis, use three periods with a space before each and put the sentence period after the final parenthesis. Thus, you will have three ellipsis points with a space before each, the closing quotation mark followed by a space, the parenthetical citation, and the period.

> R. W. B. Lewis declares that "if Hester has sinned, she has done so as an affirmation of life, and her sin is the source of life . ." (62).

Omission at the Beginning of a Sentence

Most style guides discourage the use of ellipsis points for material omitted from the beginning of a source, as shown here:

> He states: ". . . the new parent has lost the wisdom and daily support of older, more experienced family members" (Zigler 34).

The passage would read better without the ellipsis points:

> He states that "the new parent has lost the wisdom and daily support of older, more experienced family members" (Zigler 34).

Another option is this one, as stipulated by the *Chicago Manual of Style:* "If a quotation that is only part of a sentence in the original forms a complete sentence as quoted, an initial lower case letter may be changed to a capital where the structure of the text suggests it."

> He states: "The new parent has lost the wisdom and daily support of older, more experienced family members" (Zigler 34).

Here's another example:

> R. W. B. Lewis declares, "If Hester has sinned, she has done so as an affirmation of life, and her sin is the source of life . . ." (62).

Omission of Complete Sentences and Paragraphs

Use a closing punctuation mark and three spaced ellipsis points when omitting one or more sentences from within a long quotation. Here's an omission in which one sentence ends, another sentence or more is omitted, and a full sentence ends the passage.

Zigler reminds us that "child abuse is found more frequently in a single (female) parent home in which the mother is working. . . . The unavailability of quality day care can only make this situation more stressful" (42).

Here's an omission from the middle of one sentence to the middle of another:

Zigler reminds us that "child abuse is found more frequently in a single (female) parent home in which the mother is working, . . . so the unavailability of quality day care can only make this situation more stressful" (42).

Omissions in Poetry

If you omit a word or phrase in a quotation of poetry, indicate the omission with three or four ellipsis points, just as you would with omissions in a prose passage. However, if you omit a complete line or more from the poem, indicate the omission by a line of spaced periods that equals the average length of the lines. Note that the parenthetical citation shows two sets of lines.

Elizabeth Barrett Browning asks:
> Do ye hear the children weeping, O my brothers,
> Ere the sorrow comes with years
> They are leaning their young heads against their mothers,
> And that cannot stop their tears.
> . . . .
> They are weeping in the playtime of the others,
> In the country of the free. (1–4, 11–12)

Avoid Excessive Use of Ellipsis Points

Many times, you can be more effective if you incorporate short phrases rather than quote the whole sprinkled with many ellipsis points. Note how this next passage incorporates quotations without the use of ellipsis.

The long-distance marriage, according to William Nichols, "works best when there are no minor-aged children to be considered," the two people are "equipped by temperament and personality to spend a considerable amount of time alone," and both are able to "function in a mature, highly independent fashion" (54).

Ellipsis in the Original

If the original passage has ellipsis by the author, and you wish to cut additional words, place brackets around your ellipsis points to distinguish them from the author's ellipsis points. If the original says:

> Shakespeare's innovative techniques in working with revenge tragedy are important in *Hamlet* . . . while the use of a Senecan ghost is a convention of revenge tragedy, a ghost full of meaningful contradictions in calling for revenge is part of Shakespeare's dramatic suspense.

If you cut the middle phrase, use this form:

> One writer says, "Shakespeare's innovative techniques in working with revenge tragedy are important in *Hamlet* . . . [. . .] a ghost full of meaningful contradictions in calling for revenge is part of Shakespeare's dramatic suspense."

10o Altering Quotations with Parentheses and Brackets

You will sometimes need to alter a quotation to emphasize a point or to make something clear. You might add material, italicize an important word, or use the word *sic* (Latin for "thus" or "so") to alert readers that you have properly reproduced the material even though the logic or the spelling of the original might appear to be in error. Use parentheses or brackets according to these basic rules.

Parentheses

Use parentheses to enclose your comments or explanations that fall outside a quotation, shown in these examples:

> The problem with airbags is that children (even those in protective seats) can be killed by the force as the airbag explodes. Boughman (46) urges car makers to "direct the force of automotive airbags *upward* against the windshield" (emphasis added).

> Roberts (22) comments that "politicians suffer a conflict with honoure" (sic).

Brackets

Use brackets for interpolation, which means inserting your own comment into a text or quotation. The use of brackets signals the insertion. Note the following rules.

Use Brackets to Clarify

This same critic indicates that "we must avoid the temptation to read it [*The Scarlet Letter*] heretically" (118).

Use Brackets to Establish Correct Grammar within an Abridged Quotation

"John F. Kennedy [was] an immortal figure of courage and dignity in the hearts of most Americans," notes one historian (Jones 82).

He states: "[The] new parent has lost the wisdom and daily support of older, more experienced family members" (Zigler 34).

Use Brackets to Note the Addition of Underlining

He says, for instance, that the "extended family is now rare in contemporary society, and with its demise the new parent has *lost the wisdom* [my emphasis] and daily support of older, more experienced family members" (Zigler 42).

Use Brackets to Substitute a Proper Name for a Pronoun

"As we all know, he [Kennedy] implored us to serve the country, not take from it" (Jones 432).

Use Brackets with Sic to Indicate Errors in the Original

Lovell says, "John F. Kennedy, assassinated in November of 1964 [sic], became overnight an immortal figure of courage and dignity in the hearts of most Americans" (62).

> **HINT**
>
> The assassination occurred in 1963. However, do not burden your text with the use of "sic" for historical matter in which outmoded spellings are obvious, as with: "Faire seemly pleasaunce each to other makes."

Use Brackets with Ellipsis Points

See the example on pages 151–152.

Your Research Project

1. Examine your handling of the sources. Have you introduced them clearly so the reader will know when the borrowing began? Have you closed them with a page citation, as appropriate? Have you placed quotation marks at the beginning and the end of borrowed phrases as well as borrowed sentences?

2. If you have used online sources, look at them again to see if the paragraphs on the online site are numbered. If so, use the paragraph numbers in your citation(s); if not, use no numbers—not the numbers on any printout and not paragraph numbers if you must count them.

3. Look at your source material to find a table, graph, figure, or photograph you might insert into your paper as additional evidence. Be certain that you have labeled it correctly (see page 220 for an example).

4. Make a critical journey through your text to be certain you have made an informed choice about the documentation style you need. Normally, instructors will inform you. In general, use MLA style for papers in freshman composition and literature classes; use APA style for papers in the social sciences; use the footnote style for papers in history and the fine arts; use CSE number style for papers in the applied sciences.

Works Cited: MLA Style

The final step in your research project is to complete your Works Cited page. List only those materials actually used in your manuscript, including works mentioned within content endnotes and in captions to tables and illustrations. Preparing the Works Cited list will be relatively simple if you have carefully developed your working bibliography as a computer file with detailed publication data on each source cited in the paper (see pages 18–22).

Keep in mind that on occasion somebody might use your Works Cited listing for research of his or her own. The MLA documentation style gives all scholars in the field a consistent way to consult the sources. Inaccurate records might prevent an easy retracing of your steps.

Select a heading that indicates the nature of your list.

Works Cited for a list of works including books, articles, films, recordings, Internet sources, and so on that are quoted or paraphrased in the research paper.

Works Consulted if your list includes nonprint items such as an interview, letter, or speech as well as printed works.

Annotated Bibliography for a list of references that includes a description of the contents of each source (see pages 99–100).

Selected Bibliography for a list of readings on the subject.

The title "Works Cited" is usually most appropriate, because it lists scholarly works of printed books and articles, Web sources, and nonprint items.

Works pertinent to the paper but not quoted or paraphrased, such as an article on related matters, can be mentioned in a content endnote and then listed in the Works Cited.

> **NOTE**
>
> For examples of Works Cited pages, see pages 108–109 and 156–157. For an example of an annotated bibliography, see pages 99–100.

11a Formatting the Works Cited Page

Arrange items in alphabetic order by the surname of the author using the letter-by-letter system. Ignore spaces in the author's surname. Consider the first names only when two or more surnames are identical. Note how the following examples are alphabetized letter by letter. When no author is listed, alphabetize by the first important word of the title. Imagine lettered spelling for unusual items. For example, "#2 Red Dye" should be alphabetized as though it were "Number 2 Red Dye."

Dempsey, Morgan
"Facing Your Failures"
Lawrence, Jacob
Lawrence, Melissa
McPherson, James Alan
"Miracles and Tragedies in West Virginia Coal Mines"
Saint-Exupéry, Antoine de
St. James, Christopher

When two or more entries cite coauthors that begin with the same name, alphabetize by the last names of the second authors:

Huggins, Marjorie, and Devin Blythe
Huggins, Marjorie, and Stephen Fisher

The list of sources may also be divided into separate alphabetized sections for primary and secondary sources, for different media (articles, books, Internet sources), for different subject matter (biography, autobiography, letters), for different periods (Neoclassic period, Romantic period), and for different areas (German viewpoints, French viewpoints, American viewpoints).

Place the first line of each entry flush with the left margin and indent succeeding lines one-half inch. Double-space each entry as well as between all entries. Use one space after periods and other marks of punctuation.

Set the title "Works Cited" one inch down from the top of the sheet and double-space between it and the first entry. The following example illustrates a sample Works Cited page.

HINT

MLA style uses italics in place of underlining for titles.

Works Cited

Calvert, John H. "The Key Deception." *Intelligent Design Network*. 19 Oct. 2006. Web. 18 Sept. 2008.

Evans, Hestia, Lady Evans, and Dugald Steer, Eds. *Mythology*. Cambridge, MA: Candlewick, 2007. Print.

Haug, Matthew C. "Of Mice and Metaphysics: Natural Selection and Realized Population-Level Properties." *Philosophy of Science* 74.4 (2007): 431–51. Print.

Hill, Christopher T. "The Post-Scientific Society." *Issues in Science and Technology Online* 24.1 (2007). Web. 20 Sept. 2008.

Hudson, Robert G. "The Empirical Basis to Skepticism." *Minerva: An Internet Journal of Philosophy* 11 (2007). Web. 22 Sept. 2008.

Martin, Thomas R. "Religion, Myth, and Community." *An Overview of Classical Greek History from Homer to Alexander*. 3 Apr. 1999. Web. 18 Sept. 2008.

Stratton, Jerry. "Secular Humanist Pantheon." *The Biblyon Broadsheet*. 1 Apr. 2007. Web. 17 Sept. 2008.

Weisman, Alan. *The World without Us*. New York: St. Martin's, 2007. Print.

Wilson, David S. *Darwin's Cathedral: Evolution, Religion, and the Nature of Society*. Chicago: U of Chicago P, 2003. Print.

---. *Evolution for Everyone: How Darwin's Theory Can Change the Way We Think about Our Lives*. New York: Dell, 2007. Print.

INDEX TO WORKS CITED MODELS: MLA STYLE

(continued on page 158)

(continued from page 157)

INDEX TO WORKS CITED MODELS: MLA STYLE

INDEX TO WORKS CITED MODELS: MLA STYLE

(continued on page 160)

(continued from page 159)

INDEX TO WORKS CITED MODELS: MLA STYLE

11b Works Cited Form—Books

Enter information for books in the following order. Items 1, 3, 7, and 10 are required; add other items according to the circumstances explained in the text that follows.

1. Author(s)
2. Chapter or part of book
3. Title of the book
4. Editor, translator, or compiler
5. Edition
6. Volume number of book

7. Place, publisher, and date
8. Page numbers
9. Number of volumes
10. Medium of publication—"Print."

The following example shows three primary divisions of a Works Cited entry for a book—Author's Name. *Title of the Book*. Publication Information.

> Kennedy, Randall. *Sellout: The Politics of Racial Betrayal*. New York: Pantheon, 2008. Print.

Items 1, 3, 7, and 10 are always required book entries on the Works Cited page. Add other items according to the circumstances.

> Carroll, Lewis. "The Walrus and the Carpenter." *The Best Poems of the English Language*. Ed. Harold Bloom. New York: HarperCollins, 2004. 757–60. Print.

Following is a detailed breakdown of the components found in the previous entry:

> Author Name. "Title for Section of the Book." *Book Title in Italics*. Name of the editor. City, State of Publication: Name of Publisher, Year of Publication. Page Numbers. Medium of Publication.

Author's Name

List the author's name, surname first, followed by given name or initials, and then a period:

> Gingrich, Newt.

Always give authors' names in the fullest possible form, for example, "Jimmerson, Aundra V." rather than "Jimmerson, A.V," unless, as indicated on the title page of the book, the author prefers initials. If you spell out an abbreviated name, put square brackets around the material added:

> Tolkien, J[ohn] R[onald] R[euel].

With pseudonyms you may add the real name, enclosing the addition in brackets.

> Carroll, Lewis [Charles Lutwidge Dodgson].

Omit a title, affiliation, or degree that appears with the author's name on the title page.

If the title page says:	*In the Works Cited use:*
Sir John Gielgud	Gielgud, John
Sister Margaret Grayson	Grayson, Margaret
Barton O'Connor, Ph.D.	O'Connor, Barton

However, do provide an essential suffix that is part of a person's name:

Justin, Walter, Jr.
Peterson, Robert J., III.

Title of the Book

State the title of the book, including any subtitle. Use italics for the entire title, including any colon, subtitle, or punctuation. Place a period after the entire title, unless it ends in another punctuation mark.

Gingrich, Newt. *Real Change: From the World That Fails to the World That Works.*

Publication Information

Provide the city of publication, the publisher's name, the year of publication, and the medium of publication. The word *Print* is given as the medium of publication for books and periodicals.

Gingrich, Newt. *Real Change: From the World That Fails to the World That Works.* Washington, DC: Regnery, 2008. Print.

Include the abbreviation for the state or country only if necessary for clarity:

Brunstetter, Wanda E. *A Sister's Test.* Uhrichsville, OH: Barbour, 2007. Print.

If more than one place of publication appears on the title page, the first city mentioned is sufficient. If successive copyright dates are given, use the most recent (unless your study is specifically concerned with an earlier, perhaps definitive, edition). A new printing does not constitute a new edition.

If the place, publisher, date of publication, or pages are not provided, use one of these abbreviations:

n.p.	No place of publication listed
n.p.	No publisher listed
n.d.	No date of publication listed
n. pag.	No pagination listed

Lewes, George Henry. *The Life and Works of Goethe*. 1855. 2 vols. Rpt. as vols. 13 and 14 of *The Works J. W. von Goethe*. Ed. Nathan Haskell Dole. London: Nicolls, n.d. 14 vols. Print.

Provide the publisher's name in a shortened form, such as "Bobbs" rather than "Bobbs-Merrill Co., Inc." A publisher's special imprint name should be joined with the official name, for example, Anchor-Doubleday.

Miller, Sue. *The Senator's Wife*. New York: Knopf, 2008. Print.

Cite page numbers to help a reader find a particular section of a book.

Lawrence, Cooper. "The Influence of Self-Esteem." *The Cult of Perfection*. Guilford, CT: Globe Pequot, 2008. 175–97. Print.

The following list provides examples and explains the correct form for books listed on a Works Cited page.

Author, Anonymous

Begin with the title. Do not use *anonymous* or *anon*. Alphabetize by the title, ignoring initial articles, *A*, *An*, or *The*.

The Song of Roland. Trans. W. S. Merwin. New York: Random, 2006. Print.

Author, Pseudonymous but Name Supplied

Slender, Robert [Freneau, Philip]. *Letters on Various and Important Subjects*. Philadelphia: Hogan, 1799. Print.

Author, Listed by Initials with Name Supplied

Rowling, J[oanne] K[athleen]. *Harry Potter and the Deathly Hallows*. New York: Scholastic, 2007. Print.

Authors, Two

Preston, Douglas, and Lincoln Child. *The Wheel of Darkness*. New York: Warner, 2008. Print.

Authors, Three

Evans, Hestia, Lady Evans, and Dugald Steer, Eds. *Mythology*. Cambridge, MA: Candlewick, 2007. Print.

Authors, More Than Three

Use "et al.," which means "and others," or list all the authors. See the two examples that follow:

> Garrod, Andrew C., et al. *Adolescent Portraits: Identity, Relationships, and Challenges*. 6th ed. Boston: Allyn & Bacon, 2007. Print.
>
> Orlich, Donald C., Robert J. Harder, Richard C. Callahan, and Ola M. Brown. *Teaching Strategies: A Guide to Effective Instruction*. Boston: Houghton Mifflin, 2006. Print.

Author, Corporation or Institution

A corporate author can be an association, a committee, or any group or institution when the title page does not identify the names of the members.

> American Medical Association. *Health Professions Career and Education Directory 2008–2009*. New York: Random, 2008. Print.

List a committee or council as the author even when the organization is also the publisher, as in this example:

> Consumer Reports. *Consumer Reports Electronics Buying Guide 2008*. New York: Consumer Reports, 2008. Print.

Author, Two or More Books by the Same Author

When an author has two or more works, do not repeat his or her name with each entry. Rather, insert a continuous three-dash line flush with the left margin, followed by a period. Also, list the works alphabetically by the title (ignoring *a*, *an*, and *the*), not by the year of publication. In the following example, the *Wh* of *Whiteout* precedes the *Wo* of *World*.

> Follett, Ken. *Hornet Flight*. New York: New American Library, 2002. Print.
>
> ---. *Whiteout*. New York: Penguin, 2004. Print.
>
> ---. *World without End*. New York: Dutton, 2007. Print.

The three dashes stand for exactly the same name(s) as in the preceding entry. However, do not substitute three hyphens for an author who has two or more works in the Works Cited when one is written in collaboration with someone else:

> Gaiman, Neil. *Anansi Boys*. New York: HarperTorch, 2006. Print.
>
> ---. *Stardust*. New York: HarperCollins, 2007. Print.

> Gaiman, Neil, and Terry Pratchett. *Good Omens: The Nice and Accurate*
> *Prophecies of Agnes Nutter, Witch.* New York: HarperTorch, 2006. Print.

If the person edited, compiled, or translated the work that follows on the list, place a comma after the three hyphens and write *ed., comp.,* or *trans.* before you give the title. This label does not affect the alphabetic order by title.

> Finneran, Richard J., ed. *The Tower: A Facsimile Edition.* New York: Simon
> & Schuster, 2004. Print.
> ---, ed. *Yeats Reader.* New York: Scribner, 2002. Print.

Author, Two or More Books by the Same Multiple Authors

When you cite two or more books by the same authors, provide the names in the first entry only. Thereafter, use three hyphens, followed by a period.

> Axelrod, Rise B., and Charles R. Cooper. *Concise Guide to Writing.* 4th ed.
> Boston: St. Martin's, 2005. Print.
> ---. *St. Martin's Guide to Writing.* 8th ed. Boston: St. Martin's,
> 2007. Print.

Anthology, or a Compilation

In general, works in an anthology have been published previously and collected by an editor. Supply the names of authors as well as editors. Many times the prior publication data on a specific work may not be readily available; therefore, use this form:

> Glaspell, Susan. "Trifles." *The Literary Experience.* Compact Edition. Eds. Bruce
> Beiderwell and Jeffrey M. Wheeler. Boston: Thomson, Wadsworth, 2008.
> 550–61. Print.

Provide the inclusive page numbers for the piece, not just the page or pages that you have cited in the text.

> **NOTE**
>
> If you use several works from the same anthology, you can shorten the citation by citing the short work and by making cross references to the larger one; see "Cross-References to Works in a Collection," page 167.

The Bible

Do not italicize the word Bible or the books of the Bible. Common editions need no publication information, but do italicize special editions of the Bible.

The Bible. Print. [Denotes King James version]

The Geneva Bible. 1560. Facsim. rpt. Madison: U of Wisconsin P, 1961. Print.

NRSV [New Revised Standard Version] Study Bible. New York: HarperCollins, 2007. Print.

A Book Published before 1900

For older books that are now out of print, you may omit the name of the publisher and use a comma, instead of a colon, to separate the place of publication from the year. If it has no date listed, use "n.d." If it has no publisher or place of publication mentioned, use "n.p."

Dewey, John. *The School and Society.* Chicago, 1899. Print.

Chapter or Part of the Book

List the chapter or part of the book on the Works Cited page only when it is separately edited, translated, or written, or when it demands special attention. For example, if you quote from a specific chapter of a book, let's say Chapter 6 of Michael Pollan's book, the entry should read:

Pollan, Michael. *In Defense of Food.* New York: Penguin, 2008. Print.

Your in-text citation will have listed specific page numbers, so there is no reason to mention a specific chapter, even though it is the only portion of Pollan's book that you read.

NOTE

If you cite from an anthology or collection, list the title of the specific story, poem, essay, and so on. See "Anthology, or a Compilation," page 165, or "Collection, Component Part," page 166.

Classical Works

Homer. *The Odyssey.* Trans. W. H. D. Rouse. New York: Penguin, 2007. Print.

You are more likely to find a classic work in an anthology, which would require this citation:

Sophocles. *Oedipus the King. The Literary Experience.* Compact Edition. Ed. Bruce Beiderwell, and Jeffrey M. Wheeler. Boston: Thomson, Wadsworth, 2008. 64–111. Print.

Collection, Component Part

If you cite from one work in a collection of works by the same author, provide the specific name of the work and the corresponding page numbers. This next entry cites one story from a collection of stories by the same author:

Berry, Jedediah. "Inheritance." *Best New American Voices 2008*. Ed. Richard
Bausch. Orlando, FL: Harcourt, 2007. 42–57. Print.

Cross-References to Works in a Collection

If you are citing several selections from one anthology or collection, provide a full reference to the anthology (as explained on page 164) and then provide references to the individual selections by providing the author and title of the work, the last name of the editor of the collection, and the inclusive page numbers used from the anthology.

Lithgow, John, ed. *The Poet's Corner*. New York: Grand Central, 2007. Print.

Parker, Dorothy. "Afternoon." Lithgow 226–29.

Shelley, Percy Bysshe. "To a Skylark." Lithgow 193.

Wordsworth, William. "I Wandered Lonely as a Cloud." Lithgow 270.

Edition

Indicate the edition used, whenever it is not the first, in Arabic numerals ("3rd ed."), by name ("Rev. ed.," "Abr. ed."), or by year ("1999 ed."), without further punctuation:

Fenoglio-Preiser, Cecilia, et al. *Gastrointestinal Pathology: An Atlas and
Text.* 3rd ed. Philadelphia: Lippincott, Williams, & Wilkins 2008. Print.

Indicate that a work has been prepared by an editor, not the original author:

Crane, Stephen. *Maggie: A Girl of the Streets and Other Selected Stories*.
Ed. with Intro. by Alfred Kazin. New York: Signet, 2006. Print.

If you wish to show the original date of the publication, place the year immediately after the title, followed by a period. *Note:* The title of an edition in a series is capitalized.

Hardy Thomas. *Far from the Madding Crowd*. 1874. Ed. Joslyn T. Pine. Mineola,
NY: Dover, 2007. Print.

Editor, Translator, Illustrator, or Compiler

If the name of the editor or compiler appears on the title page of an anthology or compilation, place it first:

Pollack, Harriet, and Christopher Metress, eds. *Emmett Till in Literary Memory and Imagination*. Baton Rouge: Louisiana State UP, 2008. Print.

If your in-text citation refers to the work of the editor, illustrator, or translator (e.g., "The Ciardi edition caused debate among Dante scholars") use this form with the original author listed after the work, preceded by the word *By*:

Kirkpartick, Robin, trans. *The Purgatorio*. By Dante. New York: Penguin, 2008. Print.

Dore Gustave, illus. *The Raven*. By Edgar Allan Poe. Gloucester, UK: Book Depository, 2008. Print.

Kerrigan, William, Stephen M. Fallon, and John Rumrich, eds. *Complete Poetry and Essential Prose of John Milton*. New York: Random, 2007. Print.

Otherwise, mention an editor, translator, or compiler of a collection *after* the title with the abbreviations Ed., Trans., or Comp., as shown here:

Yeats, W. B. *Sophocles' Oedipus at Colonus*. Ed. Jared Curtis. Ithaca, NY: Cornell UP, 2008. Print.

Encyclopedia, Dictionary, or Reference Book

Treat works arranged alphabetically as you would an anthology or collection, but omit the name of the editor(s), the volume number, place of publication, publisher, and page number(s). If the author is listed, begin the entry with the author's name; otherwise, begin with the title of the article. If the article is signed with initials, look elsewhere in the work for a complete name. Well-known works, such as the two examples that follow, need only the edition and the year of publication.

"Tumult." *The American Heritage College Dictionary*. 4th ed. 2007. Print.

Ward, Norman. "Saskatchewan." *Encyclopedia Americana*. 2008 ed. Print.

If you cite a specific definition from among several, add *Def.* (Definition), followed by the appropriate number or letter of the definition.

"Level." Def. 4a. *The American Heritage College Dictionary*. 4th ed. 2007. Print.

Less-familiar reference works need a full citation, as shown in the next examples:

"Probiotics." *Mayo Clinic Book of Alternative Medicine*. Ed. Brent Bauer, M.D. New York: Time, 2007. Print.

"Clindamycin." *Complete Guide to Prescription and Nonprescription Drugs 2008.* Eds. H. Winter Griffith and Stephen Moore. New York: Perigee, 2008. Print.

If you cite material from a chapter of one volume in a multivolume set, you must include the volume number. Although not required, you may also provide the total number of volumes. Conform to the following entry format:

Saintsbury, George. "Dickens." *The Cambridge History of English Literature.* Ed. A. W. Ward and A. R. Waller. Vol. 13. New York: Putnam's, 1917. 14 vols. Print.

Introduction, Preface, Foreword, or Afterword

If you are citing the person who has written the introduction to a work by another author, start with the name of the person who wrote the preface or foreword. Give the name of the part being cited, neither underscored nor enclosed within quotation marks. Place the name of the author in normal order after the title preceded by the word *By.* Follow with publication information and end with the inclusive page numbers.

Wilson, E. O. Foreword. *A Contract with the Earth.* By Newt Gingrich and Terry L. Maple. Baltimore: Johns Hopkins UP, 2007. ix–x. Print.

Frantz, Sarah S. G. Introduction. *Love and Friendship.* By Jane Austin. New York: Barnes and Noble, 2007. vii–xvii. Print.

If the author has written the prefatory matter, not another person, use only the author's last name after the word *By.*

Miller, Dan. Introduction. *No More Mondays.* By Miller. New York: Currency, 2008. 1–10. Print.

Use this form only if you cite from the introduction and not the main text.

> ### NOTE
>
> For more details about this type of citation, see "Chapter or Part of the Book," page 166, and "Anthology, or a Compilation," page 165.

Manuscript or Typescript

Chaucer, Geoffrey. *The Canterbury Tales.* MS Harley 7334. British Museum, London.

Tabares, Miguel. "Voices from the Ruins of Ancient Greece."
    Unpublished essay, 2008.

Play, Classical

Shakespeare, William. *Othello*. Ed. Daniel Vitkus. Rpt. of the 1623 ed.
    Comedies, Histories, and Tragedies. New York: Barnes and Noble
    Shakespeare, 2007. Print.

Today, classical plays are usually found in anthologies, which will
require this form:

Shakespeare, William. *Hamlet*. The Literary Experience. Compact Edition. Eds.
    Bruce Beiderwell and Jeffrey M. Wheeler. Boston: Thomson, Wadsworth,
    2008. 709–817. Print.

Play, Modern

Contemporary plays may be published independently or as part of
a collection.

Shepard, Sam. *Kicking a Dead Horse*. New York: Knopf, 2008. Print.

Poem, Classical

Classical poems are usually translated, so you will often need to list a
translator and/or editor. If the work is one part of a collection, show
which anthology you used.

> **NOTE**
>
> If you cite the translator's or editor's preface or notes to the text, put the
> name of the translator or editor first. See page 173.

Dante. *The Divine Comedy*. Trans. Sean O'Brien. New York: Macmillan, 2008. Print.
Dante. *Inferno*. *The Divine Comedy*. Trans. John Ciardi.
    The Norton Anthology of World Masterpieces. Ed. Sarah Lawall et al.
    New York: Norton, 1999. 1303–1429. Print.

Poem, Modern Collection

Use this form that includes the inclusive page numbers if you cite one
short poem from a collection.

Lee, Li-Young, "Descended from Dreamers." *Behind My Eyes*. New York: Norton,
    2008. 60–61. Print.

Use this next form if you cite from one book-length poem.

Eliot, T. S. *Four Quartets. The Complete Poems and Plays 1909–1950*. New York: Harcourt, 1952. 115–45. Print.

Do not cite specific poems and pages if you cite several different poems of the collection. Your in-text citations should cite the specific poems and page numbers (see page 146). Your Works Cited entry would then list only the name of the collection.

Eliot, T. S. *The Complete Poems and Plays 1909–1950*. New York: Harcourt, 1952. Print.

Reprinted Works

Use the following form if you can quickly identify original publication information.

Tan, Amy. "Mother Tongue." *Threepenny Review* 1989: n. pag. Rpt. in *Rotten English*. Ed. Dohra Ahmad. New York: Norton, 2007. 503–10. Print.

Republished Book

If you are citing from a republished book, such as a paperback version of a book published originally in hardback, provide the original publication date after the title and then provide the publication information for the book from which you are citing.

Stevenson, Robert Louis. *Treasure Island.* 1883. Gloucester, UK: Book Depository, 2008. Print.

Although it is not required, you may wish to provide supplementary information. Give the type of reproduction to explain that the republished work is, for example, a facsimile reprinting of the text.

Laughlin, Ruth. *Caballeros: The Romance of Santa Fe and the Southwest*. 1945. Facsim. rpt. Santa Fe, NM: Sunstone, 2008. Print.

Give facts about the original publication if the information will serve the reader. In this next example the republished book was originally published under a different title.

Arnold, Matthew. "The Study of Poetry." *Essays: English and American*. Ed. Charles W. Eliot. 1886. New York: Collier, 1910. Rpt. of the General Introduction to *The English Poets*. Ed. T. H. Ward. 1880. Print.

Screenplay

Baumbach, Noah. *Margot at the Wedding: The Shooting Script.* Screenplay. New York: Newmarket, 2008. Print.

Series, Numbered and Unnumbered

If the work is one in a published series, show the name of the series, abbreviated, without quotation marks or italics, the number of this work in Arabic numerals, and a period:

> Wallerstein, Ruth C. *Richard Crashaw: A Study in Style and Poetic Development.*
> U of Wisconsin Studies in Lang. and Lit. 37. Madison: U of Wisconsin
> P, 1935. Print.

Sourcebooks and Casebooks

> Gitomer, Jeffrey. "The Secret of Self-Belief." *Little Green Book of Getting Your*
> *Way.* New York: Pearson, 2007. 20–21. Print.

If you can identify the original facts of publication, include that information also:

> Ellmann, Richard. "Reality." *Yeats: The Man and the Masks.* New York:
> Macmillan, 1948. Rpt. in *Yeats: A Collection of Critical Essays.* Ed. John
> Unterecker. Twentieth Century Views. Englewood Cliffs: Prentice, 1963.
> 163–74. Print.

NOTE

If you cite more than one article from a casebook, use cross-references. See page 167.

Title of the Book

Show the title of the work italicized, followed by a period. Separate any subtitle from the primary title by a colon and one space even though the title page has no mark of punctuation or the card catalog entry has a semicolon.

> Budiansky, Stephen. *The Bloody Shirt.* New York: Viking, 2008. Print.

If an italicized title to a book incorporates another title that normally receives italics, do not underscore or italicize the shorter title nor place it within quotation marks. In the title below, *Absalom and Acidophil* is the shorter title; it does not receive italics.

> Schilling, Bernard N. *Dryden and the Conservative Myth:*
> *A Reading of* Absalom and Acidophil. New Haven: Yale UP,
> 1961. Print.

MLA STYLE

172

Title of a Book in Another Language

In general, use lowercase letters for foreign titles except for the first major word and proper names. Provide a translation in brackets if you think it necessary (e.g., *Étranger* [*The Stranger*] or Praha [Prague]).

Eco, Umberto. *Historia de la belleza.* New York: Random House, 2007. Print.

Pauly, Daniele. *Barragan: L'espace et l'ombre, le mur et la couleur.* New York: Birkhauser Verlag, 2008. Print.

Translator

List the translator's name first only if the translator's work (preface, foreword, afterword, notes) is the focus of your study.

Marquez, Gabriel Garcia. *Memories of My Melancholy Whores.* Trans. Edith Grossman. New York: Knopf, 2005. Print.

Volumes

If you are citing from only one volume of a multivolume work, provide the number of that volume in the Works Cited entry with information for that volume only. In your text, you will need to specify only page numbers, for example, (Borgese 45–51).

Chircop, Aldo, Moira L. McConnell, and Scott Coffen-Smout, eds. *Ocean Yearbook.* Vol. 22. Chicago: U of Chicago P, 2008. Print.

Although additional information is not required, you may provide the inclusive page numbers, the total number of volumes, and the inclusive dates of publication.

Lauter, Paul, ed. "New Generations: Postmodernity and Difference." *The Heath Anthology of American Literature.* 5th ed. Vol. E. Boston: Houghton Mifflin, 2006. 2345–54. 5 vols. Print.

If you are citing from two or more volumes of a multivolume work, your in-text citation will need to specify volume and page (2: 120–121); then the Works Cited entry will need to show the total number of volumes in Arabic numerals, as shown here.

Hersen, Michel. *Handbook of Psychological Assessment, Case Conceptualization, and Treatment.* 2 vols. Indianapolis: Wiley, 2007. Print.

If you are citing from volumes that were published over a period of years, provide the inclusive dates at the end of the citation. Should the volumes still be in production, write *to date* after the number of volumes and leave a space after the dash that follows the initial date.

Walsch, Neale Donald. *Conversations with God: An Uncommon Dialogue.* 3 vols.
New York: Penguin, 1996–98. Print.

Cassidy, Frederic, ed. *Dictionary of American Regional English.*
3 vols. to date. Cambridge: Belknap-Harvard UP, 1985– . Print.

If you are using only one volume of a multivolume work and the volume has an individual title, you can cite the one work without mentioning the other volumes in the set.

Crane, Stephen. *Wounds in the Rain. Stephen Crane: Tales of War.*
Charlottesville: UP of Virginia, 1970. 95–284. Print.

As a courtesy to the reader, you may include supplementary information about an entire edition.

Crane, Stephen. *Wounds in the Rain. Stephen Crane: Tales of War.*
Charlottesville: UP of Virginia, 1970. Vol. 6 of *The University of Virginia Edition of the Works of Stephen Crane.* Ed. Fredson Bowers. 95–284.
10 vols. 1969–76. Print.

11c Works Cited Form—Periodicals

For journal or magazine articles, use the following order:

1. Author(s)
2. Title of the article
3. Name of the periodical—*italicized*
4. Series number (if it is relevant)
5. Volume and issue number (for journals)—(e.g., 70.4)
6. Date of publication
7. Page numbers
8. Medium of publication—"Print."

Lindberg, Erik. "Expert Energy-saving Tips." *The Family Handyman* June 2008:
44–46. Print.

Following is a detailed breakdown of the components found in the previous entry:

Author's Name. "Title of Article." *Title of Periodical* Publication Date: Page
Numbers. Medium of Publication.

Give the name of the journal or magazine in full, italicized, and with no following punctuation. Omit any introductory article, such as *The.*

Panning, Anne. "All-U-Can-Eat." Kenyon Review 29.4 (Fall 2007):
    21–40. Print.

Be sure to include the volume as well as issue number for journals immediately after the title of the journal. In this example, the volume and issue number is 29.4. If no issue number is provided, then simply give the volume number, 29, for example. Magazine entries on the Works Cited page do not need to mention the volume or issue number because they are usually printed on a weekly basis; hence, the date is more useful for locating a magazine article.

The formatting of Works Cited entries for periodicals are explained and illustrated in the following examples.

Abstract in an Abstracts Journal

If you have cited from an abstract found in a journal devoted to abstracts, not full articles, begin the citation with information on the original work and then give information on the abstracts journal. Use either item number or page number according to how the journal provides the abstracts.

Gabriel, Adrian T., Timm Meyer, and Guido Germano. "Molecular Graphics of
    Convex Body Fluids." *Journal of Chemistry Theory and Computation* 70.3
    (2008): 192–93. *Chemical Abstracts* 101 (2008): item 5523. Print.

Add the word *Abstract* if the title does not make clear that you have used an abstract, not a full article.

Crowell, Sheila E., et al. "Parent-Child Interactions, Peripheral Serotonin, and
    Self-inflicted Injury in Adolescents." *Journal of Consulting and Clinical
    Psychology* 76.1 (2008): 15–21. Abstract. PsycLIT 2008:18544. Print.

Use the next form when you cite from *Dissertation Abstracts International (DAI)*. The page number features A, B, or C to designate the series used: A—Humanities, B—Sciences, C—European dissertations. Before volume 30 (1969) the title was *Dissertation Abstracts*, so use *DA* for those early volumes.

Nicholson, Andre Wesley. "Criticisms and Critiques: An Analysis of Proofreading
    Marks of College English Professors." Diss. Southern Tech. U, 2008.
    DAI 66 (2008): 2957D. Print.

Author(s)

Show the author's name flush with the left margin, without a numeral and with succeeding lines indented five spaces. Enter the surname first, followed by a comma, followed by a given name or initials, followed by a period:

> Kleine-Ahlbrandt, Stephanie, and Andrew Small. "China's New
> Dictatorship Diplomacy." *Foreign Affairs* 87.1 (Jan./Feb. 2008):
> 38–56. Print.

Author, Anonymous

> "Italy." *Biblical Archeology Review* Jan./Feb. 2008: 88. Print.

Interview, Published

> Rosenfeld, Jordan E. Interview with Tess Gerritsen. "Mistress of Suspense."
> *Writer's Digest* Feb. 2008: 50–55. Print.

Journal, with All Issues for a Year Paged Continuously

> Pavalko, Eliza K., Fang Gong, and J. Scott Long. "Women's Work, Cohort
> Change, and Health." *Journal of Health & Social Behavior* 48.4 (2007):
> 352–68. Print.

Journal, with Each Issue Paged Anew

Add the issue number after the volume number, because page numbers alone are not sufficient to locate the article within a volume of six or 12 issues when each issue has separate pagination. Adding the month or season with the year will also serve the researcher.

> McCorkle, Jill. "Cuss Time." *The American Scholar* 77.1 (Win. 2008):
> 59–62. Print.

If a journal uses only an issue number, treat it as a volume number:

> Michta, Andrew A. "Double or Nothing." *The National Interest* 93 (Jan./Feb.
> 2008): 54–57. Print.

Loose-Leaf Collection

> Clemmitt, Marcia. "Climate Change." *CQ Researcher* 16.4 (27 Jan. 2006):
> 75+. Print.

Magazine

With magazines, the volume number offers little help for finding an article. For example, one volume of *Time* (52 issues) will have page 16 repeated 52 times. For this reason, you need to insert an exact date (month and day) for weekly and fortnightly (every two weeks) publications. Do not list the volume and issue numbers.

> Le Guin, Ursula K. "Staying Awake." *Harper's* Feb. 2008: 76–84. Print.

The month suffices for monthly and bimonthly publications:

> Lobel, Hannah. "Shame on Us." Utne Jan./Feb. 2008: 36–37. Print.

Microform

Some reference sources, such as *NewsBank*, republish articles on microfiche. If you use such a microform, enter the original publication information first and then add the pertinent information about the microform, as shown.

> Chapman, Dan. "Panel Could Help Protect Children." *Winston-Salem Journal* 14
> Jan. 1990: 14. Microform. *Newsbank: Welfare and Social Problems* 12
> (1990): fiche 1, grids A8–11.

Notes, Editorials, Queries, Reports, Comments, and Letters

Magazines and journals publish many pieces that are not full-fledged articles. Identify this type of material if the title of the article or the name of the journal does not make clear the nature of the material (e.g., "Letter" or "Comment").

> Maltby, Richard E., Jr. "Be My Valentine: Heart Transplants." Puzzle. *Harper's*
> Feb. 2008: 95. Print.
> Perina, Kaja. "Waiting for Attraction to Strike." Editor's note. *Psychology Today*
> 41.1 (Jan./Feb. 2008): 7. Print.
> Waring-Flood, Clive. "Market Changes." Editorial. *Silvershotz* 4.4 (2007): 2. Print.

Reprint of a Journal Article

> Vail, Kathleen. "Climate Control." *American School Board Journal* 192.6 (June
> 2005): 12–19. Print. *Education Digest* Dec. 2005: 4–11.

Review, in a Magazine, Newspaper, or Journal

Name the reviewer and the title of the review. Then write *Rev. of* and the title of the work being reviewed, followed by a comma, and the name of the author or producer. If necessary, identify the nature of the work within brackets immediately after the title.

> Macowlay, Scott. "Wrong Turn." Rev. of *Taxi to the Dark Side,* by Alex Gibney.
> *Filmmaker.* 16.2 (Win. 2008): 56+. Print.

If the name of the reviewer is not provided, begin the entry with the title of the review.

"Nikon D300: A New Standard?" Rev. of Nikon D300. *Photography Monthly* Feb. 2008: 96+. Print.

If the review has no title, omit it from the entry.

Benedict-Nelson, Andrew. Rev. of *The Summer Isles,* by Ian R. MacLeod. *Bookmarks* 32 (Jan./Feb. 2008): 19. Print.

Skipped Pages in an Article

Supply inclusive page numbers (202–09, 85–115, or 1112–24), but if an article is paged here and there throughout the issue (for example, pages 74, 78, and 81–88), write only the first page number and a plus sign with no intervening space.

Larson, Christine. "Keeping Your Brain Fit." *U.S. News & World Report* 11 Feb. 2008: 41+. Print.

Special Issue

If you cite one article from a special issue of a journal, you may indicate the nature of this special issue, as shown next.

Bedusa, Jennie. "Photographer Focus: Connie Imboden." *Focus.* Spec. Issue of *Focus* 15 (Feb. 2008): 72–79. Print

If you cite several articles from the special issue, begin the primary citation with the name of the editor.

Perloff, Stephen, ed. Spec. Issue of *Focus* 15 (Feb. 2008): 1–209. Print.

When that entry is established, cross-reference each article used in the following manner.

Lambert, Patricia. "Bet's Bench." Photograph. *Perloff,* 119.

NOTE

See also "Cross-References to Works in a Collection," page 167.

Speech or Address, Published

United States. President. "State of the Union." *Weekly Compilation of Presidential Documents* pd04fe08 txt-11 (1 Feb. 2008): 117–25. Print.

Title of the Article

Show the title within quotation marks followed by a period inside the closing quotation marks.

Theil, Stefan. "Europe's Philosophy of Failure." *Foreign Policy* (Jan./Feb. 2008): 54–60. Print.

Title, Omitted

Granderson, Milton. *Oakleaf Journal of Conservation* 23.3 (2008): 93–94. Print.

Title, within the Article's Title

Rammelkamp, Charles. "Origins of Shakespeare's *Romeo and Juliet*." *Renaissance* 13.1 (Issue #59): 42–44. Print.

Title, Foreign

Correa, Armando, and Maria Morales. "La Importancia de Ser." *People en Espanol* Diciembre/Enero 2006: 136–41. Print.

> **NOTE**
>
> See also "Title of a Book in Another Language," page 173.

179

Volume, Issue, and Page Numbers for Journals

Some journals are paged continuously through all issues of an entire year, so listing the month of publication is unnecessary. For clarity, provide the volume and issue number, as well as the page numbers. Give the issue number following the volume number, separated by a period.

Greenspoon, Leonard J. "Casting Pearls before Swine." *Biblical Archeology Review* 34.1 (Jan./Feb. 2008): 13. Print.

11d Works Cited Form—Newspapers

Provide the name of the author, the title of the article, and the name of the newspaper as it appears on the masthead, omitting any introductory article (e.g., *Wall Street Journal*, not *The Wall Street Journal*). If the city of publication is not included in the name of a newspaper published locally, add the city in square brackets, not italicized, after the name: "*Times-Picayune* [New Orleans]." Provide the complete date—day, month (abbreviated), and year. Omit any volume and issue numbers.

Provide a page number as listed (e.g., 21, B-7, 13C, D4). For example, *USA Today* uses "6A" but the *New York Times* uses "A6." There is no uniformity among newspapers on this matter, so list the page accurately as an aid to your reader. If the article is not printed on consecutive pages, for example, if it begins on page 1 and skips to page 8, write the first page number and a plus (+) sign (see the entry below). Finally, provide the medium of publication—"Print."

Newspaper in One Section

Samuels, Christina A. "Embracing 'Response to Intervention.'" *Education Week* 23 Jan. 2008: 23–24. Print.

Newspaper with Lettered Sections

Kaufman, Marc, and Josh White. "Bull's-eye: Navy Missle Scores Hit on Falling Satellite." *Denver Post* 21 Feb. 2008: 1A+. Print.

Newspaper with Numbered Sections

Berger, Susan. "Animal Rescuers, Officials Clash." *Chicago Tribune* 26 Nov. 2005, sec. 1: 1. Print.

Newspaper Editorial with No Author Listed

"Stifling Online Speech." Editorial. *New York Times* 21 Feb. 2008: A22. Print.

Newspaper Column, Cartoon, Comic Strip, or Advertisement

Add a description to the entry to explain that the citation refers to something other than a regular news story.

Williams, Dick. "Honesty for Taxpayers." Column. *Atlanta Business Chronicle* 15 Feb. 2008: 26A. Print.

Newspaper Article with City Added

In the case of locally published newspapers, add the city in square brackets (see also the sample entry immediately above).

Kuyper, Tom. "Giving Awards Does Have a Special Value in Youth Sports." *Leaf Chronicle* [Clarksville, TN] 2 July 2008: C1. Print.

Newspaper Edition or Section

When the masthead lists an edition, add a comma after the date and name the edition (*late ed., city ed.*), followed by a colon and then the page number.

Feagans, Brian. "True Feel for the Circus." *Atlanta Journal-Constitution* 21 Feb. 2008, home ed.: A1+. Print.

Newspaper in a Foreign Language

"Les Grands de ce monde reunis a Saint-Petersbourg." *Le Monde* 30 mai 2003: 1. Print.

11e Works Cited Form — Government Documents

Since the nature of public documents is so varied, the form of the entry cannot be standardized. Therefore, you should provide sufficient information so that the reader can easily locate the reference. As a general rule, place information in the Works Cited entry in this order (but see below if you know the author, editor, or compiler of the document):

1. Government
2. Body or agency
3. Subsidiary body
4. Title of document
5. Identifying numbers
6. Publication facts
7. Medium of publication

When you cite two or more works by the same government, substitute three hyphens for the name of each government or body that you repeat:

United States. Cong. House.

---. ---. Senate.

---. Dept. of Justice.

Congressional Papers

Senate and House sections are identified by an S or an H with document numbers (e.g., S. Res. 16) and page numbers (e.g., H2345–47).

United States. Cong. Senate. *Natural Resource Protection Cooperative Agreement Act*. 110th Cong., 1st sess. S. Bill 110–10. Washington, DC: GPO, 2007. Print.

---. ---. ---. *911 Modernization Act*. 110th Cong., 1st sess. S. Bill 110–38. Washington, DC: GPO, 2007. Print.

If you provide a citation to the *Congressional Record*, you should abbreviate it and provide only the date and page numbers.

> *Cong. Rec.* 13 Feb. 2008: S937–57. Print.

Executive Branch Documents

> United States. Dept. of State. *Foreign Relations of the United States: Diplomatic Papers, 1943.* 5 vols. Washington, DC: GPO, 1943–44. Print.
>
> ---. President. *2008 Economic Report of the President.* Washington, DC: GPO, 2008. Print.

Documents of State Governments

Publication information on state papers will vary widely, so provide sufficient data for your reader to find the document.

> *2007–2008 Statistical Report.* Nashville: Tennessee Board of Regents, 2008. TBR A-001-03. Print.
>
> *Tennessee Election Returns, 1796–1825.* Microfilm. Nashville: Tennessee State Library and Archives, n.d. M-Film JK 5292 T46. Print.
>
> "Giles County." *2006–07 Directory of Public Schools.* Nashville: State Dept. of Educ., n.d. 61. Print.

Legal Citations and Public Statutes

Use the following examples as guidelines for developing your citations, which can usually appear as parenthetical citations in your text, but not on the Works Cited page.

> Illinois. Revised Statutes Annotated. Sec. 16-7-81. 2008. Print.
>
> Noise Control Act of 2007. Pub. L. 92–574. 2007. Stat. 86. Print.
>
> People v. McIntosh. California 321 P.3d 876, 2001–6. 1970. Print.
>
> State v. Lane. Minnesota 263 N. W. 608. 1935. Print.
>
> U.S. Const. Art. 2, sec. 1. Print.

11f Works Cited Form—Internet Sources

Modern technology makes it possible for you to have access to information at your computer. In particular, the Internet opens a cornucopia of information from millions of sources. Other electronic sources include e-mail and databases.

Because of their length and the fluid changes of the network, the *MLA Style Manual,* 3rd edition, no longer recommends the inclusion of URLs in the Works Cited entries for Web publications. Instead, researchers may document the medium of documentation by providing the word "Web," followed by a period, just before the date of access. Rather than typing the URL, readers are now more likely to find resources on the Web by searching for the name of the author or the title of the article. This streamlining of entries will benefit the researcher while still allowing the reader the necessary documentation information for the source.

Citing Sources Found on the Internet

Include these items as appropriate to the source:

1. Author/editor name
2. Title of the article within quotation marks, or the title of a posting to a discussion list or forum followed by the words *online posting,* followed by a period
3. Publication information and the date of document's printed version
4. Information on the electronic publication, such as the title of the site, the date of the posting, and the sponsoring organization, followed by a period
5. The medium of publication—"Web"
6. Date of your access, followed by a period

> **NOTE**
>
> For discussion of the Internet's special format, see pages 38–50. For making judgments about the validity of Internet sources, see pages 50–51.

> **NOTE**
>
> Do not include page numbers unless the Internet article shows original page numbers from the printed version of the journal or magazine. Do not include the total number of paragraphs nor specific paragraph numbers unless the original Internet article has provided them.

World Wide Web Sites

Titles of books and journals from online sources should be shown in italics.

Abstract

Brown, Gregory G., et al. "Performance of Schizophrenia and Bipolar Patients on Verbal and Figural Working Memory Tasks." Abstract. *Journal of Abnormal Psychology* 116.4 (2007): 741. Web. 10 May 2008.

Advertisement

"R.M.S. Titanic, Inc." Advertisement. Arizona Science Center, 2008. Web. 14 Feb. 2008.

Anonymous Article

"What's Your PSI? Test Your Tire Safety Knowledge." *National Highway Traffic Safety Administration*. NHTSA, n.d. Web. 23 Sept. 2008.

Archive or Scholarly Project

British Poetry Archive. Ed. Jerome McGann and David Seaman. U of Virginia Lib, 2006. Web. 19 Apr. 2008.

Article from an Online Magazine

"Controlling Anger—Before It Controls You." *APA Online.* American Psychological Association, 10 May 2008. Web. 30 Sept. 2008.

Article from a Scholarly Journal

Osilla, Karen Chan, et al. "A Brief Intervention for At-Risk Drinking in an Employee Assistance Program." *Journal of Studies on Alcohol and Drugs* 69 (2008): 14–20. Web. 2 Dec. 2008.

Article Written for the Internet

"History of Elba." *Elba on line,* 2008. Web. 12 Apr. 2008.

Audio Program Online

See the entry for "Television or Radio Program," page 188.

Blogs and Chat Rooms

Carella, Lucinda, narr. "Speaking to an Elderly Parent." *Medhealth Metapage.* Medical Health and Resources, 13 Sept. 2008. Web. 28 Oct. 2008.

Chat rooms seldom have great value, but on occasion you might find something that you wish to cite; if so, use this form.

"Weight Loss Support." *Yahoo! Chat.* Yahoo, 30 May 2008. Web. 4 Oct. 2008.

Cartoon

Parker, Brant. "How Come You Don't Celebrate Valentine's Day?" Cartoon.
Wizard of Id. 14 Feb. 2008. Web. 29 Feb. 2008.

Chapter or Portion of a Book

Add the name of the chapter after the author's name.

Dewey, John. "Waste in Education." *School and Society*. Chicago: U of Chicago
P, 1907. Web. 14 Sept. 2008.

Database

Most libraries subscribe to online databases, such as Lexis-Nexis,
ProQuest Direct, EBSCOhost, Electric Library, InfoTrac, and others.
Omit the identifying numbers for the database or the key term used in
the search. Following are examples.

"America's Children: Key National Indicators of Well-Being, 2007." Federal
Interagency Forum on Child and Family Statistics. 2007. *ERIC*. Web.
8 Dec. 2008.

Brezina, Timothy. "Teenage Violence toward Parents as an Adaptation to Family
Strain: Evidence from a National Survey of Male Adolescents." *Youth and
Society* 30 (1999): 416–44. *MasterFILE Elite*. Clarksville Montgomery
County Library, Clarksville, TN. Web. 23 Feb. 2008.

Esslin, Martin. "Theater of the Absurd." *Grolier Multimedia Encyclopedia*. 2007
ed. Web. 22 Oct. 2007.

Lee, Catherine C. "The South in Toni Morrison's *Song of Solomon*: Initiation,
Healing, and Home." *Studies in the Literary Imagination* 31 (1998):
109–23. *InfoTrac*. Web. 19 Sept. 2008.

Sloan, T. A. "Pilates: Your Ticket to a Longer, Leaner You." *Discovery Health*,
30 Oct. 2007. *EBSCOhost*. Web. 23 Jan. 2008.

Editorial

Elliott, Jim. "Fear Mongering Undermines U.S. Constitution." Editorial. *Billings
Outpost Online*, 21 Feb. 2008. Web. 21 Feb. 2008.

E-mail

Wright, Ellen. "Online Composition Courses." Message to the author.
24 May 2008. E-mail.

Encyclopedia Article Online

"Kurt Vonnegut, Jr." *Encyclopedia Britannica Online*. Encyclopedia Britannica,
2007. Web. 9 Nov. 2007.

Film or Video Online

"Epiphany: Festival of Lights." *The History of the Orthodox Christian Church*.
GoTelecom Online, 2008. Web. 24 Oct. 2008.

Home Page for an Academic Course

Wilkins, John, Trisch Longbrake, and Tom Barrett. "Uses of Science in Society."
Dept. of Physics, Ohio State U, 15 Dec. 2007. Web. 12 Jan. 2008.

Home Page for an Academic Department

"Department of Lauguage and Literature." Home page. Dept. of
Language and Literature, Clayton State U, 2008. Web.
12 Sept. 2008.

Home Page for an Academic Site

When citing a specific article from a home page, provide a Works Cited entry.

"Robert Penn Warren: 1905–1989." Home page. *Modern American
Poetry*, Dept. of English, U of Illinois, Urbana-Champaign, 2008.
Web. 2 Apr. 2008.

Home Page for a Personal Web Site

Giovanni, Nikki. Home Page. Dept. of English, Virginia Tech U, 2008. Web.
2 Apr. 2008.

Interview

Kowars, Kacey. Interview with Pete Hamill, author of *North River*. *Kacey Kowars
Show*, 18 Jul. 2007. Web. 24 Mar. 2008.

Journal Article

Stillar, Scott. "Shocking the Cultureless: The Crucial Role of Culture Shock in
Racial Identity Transformation." *Electronic Journal of Sociology* (2007):
1–16. Web. 22 Jan. 2008.

Manuscript

Girondo, Oliverio. *Scarecrow & Other Anomalies*. Trans. Gilbert Alter-Gilbert.
MS. 2002. Web. 24 Aug. 2008.

Map

"Virginia—1735." Map. *U.S. County Formation Maps, 1643–Present*. Genealogy,
Inc., 1999. Web. 24 Sept. 2008.

Newsletter

Oswald, Tom. "Tobacco Smoke Linked to Workplace Death." *MSU News Bulletin* 39.12 (21 Feb. 2008). Web. 28 Feb. 2008.

Newspaper Article, Column, or Editorial

Tettamanti, Maria. "Boulevard of Dreams." *Miamiherald.com*. Miami Herald, 22 Feb. 2008. Web. 28 Feb. 2008.

Novel

Conrad, Joseph. "Chapter 1." *Heart of Darkness*. 1902. Web. 26 Sept. 2008.

Online Posting for E-mail Discussion Groups

Supply the name of the list's moderator and the Internet site, if known; otherwise show the e-mail address of the list's moderator.

Chapman, David. "An Electoral System for Iraq." Online Posting. Democracy Design Forum, 21 June 2005. Web. 27 Nov. 2008.

Photo, Painting, or Sculpture

MLA style does not require you to label the type of work, as shown in the example of a photograph. Usually, the text will have established the nature of the work. However, if you feel that clarification is necessary, as in the case of "The Blessed Damozel," which is both a painting and a poem, you may wish to designate the form.

"Boy and Bear." Bronze sculpture. Marshall M. Fredericks Sculpture Museum, 2007. Web. 29 Aug. 2008.

Joscelyn, Steven. "Leadenhall Market." Photograph. *Pbase*, 2008. Web. 12 Aug. 2008.

Rossetti, Dante. "The Blessed Damozel." 1875–78. Painting. *Rossetti Archive*, 2008. Web. 30 Sept. 2008.

Poem, Song, or Story

Dylan, Bob. "Tangled Up in Blue." 1975. Song lyrics. *BobDylan.com*, 2008. Web. 13 Mar. 2008.

Hardy, Thomas. "To a Lady." *Wessex Poems and Other Verses*. 1898. *Project Bartleby*. Great Books Online, 2008. Web. 10 Oct. 2008.

Report

"Spam Summit: The Next Generation of Threats and Solutions." Federal Trade Commission, Nov. 2007. Web. 4 Dec. 2007.

Serialized Article

Brenner, Sydney. "The Next 100 Years of Biology." The Discovery Lecture Series.
Vanderbilt Medical Center, 14 Sept. 2006. Web. 20 Oct. 2008.

Song

See "Poem, Song, or Story" on page 187.

Sound Clip, Speech, or Recording

See "Television or Radio Program" on page 188.

Story

See "Poem, Song, or Story" on page 187.

Television or Radio Program

Simon, Scott. "Bhangra's DJ Rekha Takes the Dance Floor." *Weekend Edition*.
National Public Radio, 16 Feb. 2008. Web. 9 Mar. 2008.

University Posting, Online Article

Wetterich, Chris. "Smoke Free." Online posting. U of Illinois at Springfield, Feb.
2008. Web. 28 Feb. 2008.

Video

See "Film or Video Online," page 186.

11g Works Cited Form—Citing CD-ROM and Database Sources

CD-ROM technology provides information in four different ways, and each method of transmission requires an adjustment in the form of the entry for your Works Cited page.

Full-Text Articles with Publication Information for the Printed Source

Full-text articles are available from national distributors, such as Gale Cengage (InfoTrac), UMI-ProQuest (ProQuest), Silverplatter, or SIRS CD-ROM Information Systems. (*Note:* Most of these sources are also available online.) Conform to the examples that follow.

Brand, Madeleine. "Walking the Immigration Line." *National Public Radio.*
NPR, 24 Jan. 2008. CD-ROM. *EBSCOhost.* EBSCOhost Research Database,
May 2008.

Weise, Elizabeth. "Agreement Could Bring End to Animal Testing." *USA Today* 14
Feb. 2008: n.p. CD-ROM. *SIRS Researcher.* Boca Raton, FL: SIRS, 2008.

NOTE

See also page 194 for citing SIRS in its loose-leaf form.

HINT

Complete information may not be readily available; for example, the
original publication data may be missing. In such cases, provide what
is available.

"Nor Any Drop to Drink." *Economist* 385 (8 Dec. 2007): 41. CD-ROM.
EBSCOhost. EBSCOhost Research Database, May 2008.

Full-Text Articles with No Publication Information for a Printed Source

Sometimes the original printed source of an article or report will not
be provided by the distributor of the CD-ROM database. In such a case,
conform to the examples that follow, which provide limited data.

"Faulkner Biography." *Discovering Authors.* CD-ROM. Farmington Hills,
MI: Gale, 2008.

"U.S. Population by Age: Urban and Urbanized Areas." *2007 U.S. Census
Bureau.* CD-ROM. US Bureau of the Census. 2007.

Complete Books and Other Publications on CD-ROM

Cite this type of source as you would a book, and then provide information to the electronic source that you accessed.

The Bible. Life Application Study Bible. CD-ROM. Carol Stream, IL: Tyndale
House, 2007.

English Poetry Full-Text Database. Rel. 2. CD-ROM. Cambridge, Eng.: Chadwyck, 2008.

"John F. Kennedy." *InfoPedia.* CD-ROM. N.p.: Future Vision, n.d.

Poe, Edgar Allan. "Fall of the House of Usher." *Electronic Classical Library.*
CD-ROM. Garden Grove, CA: World Library, 2007.

Abstracts to Books and Articles Provided by the National Distributors

As a service to readers, the national distributors have members of their staff write abstracts of articles and books if the original authors have not provided such abstracts. As a result, an abstract that you find on InfoTrac and ProQuest may not be written by the original author, so you should not quote such abstracts. You may quote from abstracts that say, "Abstract written by the author." Some databases *do* have abstracts written by the original authors. In either case, you need to show in the Works Cited entry that you have cited from the abstract, so conform to the example that follows, which provides name, title, publication information, the word *abstract*, the name of the database italicized, the medium (CD-ROM), the name of the vendor, and—if available to you—the electronic publication date (month and year).

> Peekhaus, Wilhelm. "Privacy for Sale—Business as Usual in the 21st Century: An Economic and Normative Critique." *Journal of Information Ethics* 16.1 (Spring 2007): 83–98. Abstract. CD-ROM. *EBSCOhost.* 29 Jan. 2008.

Nonperiodical Publication on CD-ROM or Diskette

Cite a CD-ROM, diskette, or cassette tape as you would for a book with the addition of a descriptive word. If relevant, show the edition (3rd ed.), release (Rel. 2), or version (Ver. 3). Conform to the examples that follow:

> Lester, James D., Jr. *Introduction to Greek Mythology: Computer Slide Show.* 12 lessons on CD-ROM. Morrow, GA: Clayton State U, 2008.
>
> *2007 Statistics on Child Abuse—Montgomery County, Tennessee.* Rel. 2. Diskette. Clarksville, TN: Harriett Cohn Mental Health Center, 2008.

Encyclopedia Article

For an encyclopedia article on a compact disc, use the following form.

> "Abolitionist Movement." *Compton's Interactive Encyclopedia.* CD-ROM. The Learning Company, 2007.

Multidisc Publication

When citing a multidisc publication, follow the term CD-ROM with the total number of discs or with the disc that you cited from.

Springer, Alice G. *Barron's AP Spanish—2008*. 6th ed. CD-ROM. Disc 3.
Hauppauge, NY: Barron's, 2008.

11h Works Cited Form—Other Electronic Sources

Citing a Source That You Access in More Than One Medium

Some distributors issue packages that include different media, such as CD-ROM and accompanying microfiche or a diskette and an accompanying videotape. Cite such publications as you would a nonperiodical CD-ROM (see "Multidisc Publication," page 190) with the addition of the media available with this product.

Franking, Holly. *The Martensville Nightmare*. Ver. 1.0. Diskette. CD-ROM. Prairie
Village, KS: Diskotech, 2005.

Silver, Daniel J. "The Battle of the Books." Rev. of *The Western Canon: The
Books and School of the Ages*, by Harold Bloom. CD-ROM. *Resource/One*.
UMI-ProQuest. Feb. 1995.

Chaucer, Geoffrey. "Prologue." *Canterbury Tales*. Videocassette. CD-ROM.
Princeton, NJ: Films for the Humanities and Sciences, 2006.

191

11i Works Cited Form—Other Sources

Advertisement

Provide the title of the advertisement, within quotation marks, or the name of the product or company, not within quotation marks, the label "Advertisement" and publication information.

"Teaching for Intelligence: Believe to Achieve Conference." Advertisement.
Education Week, 23 Jan. 2008: 2. Print.

OnStar. Advertisement. CNN. 4 Aug. 2008. Television.

Art Work

If you actually experience the work itself, use the following form.

Remington, Frederic. *Mountain Man*. Bronze sculpture. Metropolitan Museum of
Art, New York. Visual art.

If the art work is a special showing at a museum, use the form of this next example.

Sloan, John. "Seeing the City: Sloan's New York." Art Exhibition. Westmoreland
Museum of American Art, Greensburg, PA. 27 Feb. 2008. Visual art.

"Beth Campbell: Following Room." Whitney Museum of American Art, New York.
10 Feb. 2008. Visual art.

Use this next form to cite reproductions in books and journals.

Raphael. *School of Athens*. The Vatican, Rome. *The World Book-Encyclopedia*,
2007 ed. Print.

If you show the date of the original, place the date immediately
after the title.

Raphael. *School of Athens*. 1510–1511. The Vatican, Rome. *The World Book-
Encyclopedia*. 2007 ed. Print.

Broadcast Interview

Reed, Philip. "Car Loans." Interview. CNN. 23 Feb. 2008. Television.

Bulletin

South Carolina Market Bulletin. Columbia, SC: South Carolina Department
of Agriculture, 21 Feb. 2008. Print.
Maryland State Bar Association's Public Awareness Committee.
Appointing a Guardian. Baltimore: Maryland State Bar Association.
2008. Print.

Cartoon

If you cannot decipher the name of the cartoonist and cannot find a
title, use this form.

Cartoon. *Education Week* 23 Jan. 2008: 36. Print.

Sometimes you will have the artist's name but not the name of
the cartoon.

Rickert, David. Cartoon. *English Journal* Jan. 2008: 94. Print.

Some cartoons are reprinted in magazines.

Ramirez. "Peace." Cartoon. Rpt. in *Weekly Standard* 2 June 2005: 13. Print.

Computer Software

Publisher Deluxe 2007. Redmond, WA: Microsoft, 2007. CD-ROM.

Conference Proceedings

Caunt-Nulton, Heather, Samantha Kulatilake, and I-hao Woo, eds.
*BUCLD-31: Proceedings of the Thirty-first Boston University
Conference on Language Development.* Apr. 2007. Somerville, MA:
Cascadilla, 2007. Print.

Dissertation, Published

Wu, Zhaohong. *Automated Optimal Design of Dynamic Systems.* Diss. U
Texas at Austin, 2007. Austin: U Texas, 2007. Print.

Dissertation, Unpublished

Patel-McCune, Santha. "An Analysis of Homophone Errors in the Writing
of 7th Grade Language Arts Students: Implications for Middle School
Teachers." Diss. Southern Tech. U, 2008. Print.

> **NOTE**
>
> If you cite only the abstract of a dissertation, see "Abstract in an
> Abstracts Journal," page 175, for the correct form.

OTHER SOURCES

Film, Videocassette, or DVD

Cite the title of a film, the director, the distributor, and the year.

Harry Potter and the Half-Blood Prince. Dir. David Yates. Warner Bros. Video,
2008. DVD.

If relevant to your study, add the names of performers, writers, or
producers after the name of the director.

Juno. Dir. Jason Reitman. Screenplay by Diablo Cody. Newmarket,
2008. DVD.

If the film is a DVD, videocassette, filmstrip, slide program, or
videodisc, add the type of publication medium after the date. You can
also add the date of the original film, if relevant.

Crimmins, Morton. "Robert Lowell—American Poet." Lecture. Western
State U, 2007. Videocassette.
Citizen Kane. Dir. Orson Welles. 1941. Warner, 2002. DVD.

If you are citing the accomplishments of the director or a performer, begin the citation with that person's name.

Caird, John, and Gavin Taylor, dir. *Les Miserables*. 1995. Perf. Colm
Wilkinson, Philip Quast, Ruthie Henshall, and Jenny Galloway. BBC,
2008. DVD.

If you cannot find certain information, such as the original date
of the film, cite what is available.

Altman, Robert, dir. *The Room*. Perf. Julian Sands, Linda Hunt, and Annie
Lennox. Prism. Videocassette.

Interview, Unpublished

For an interview that you conduct, name the person interviewed, the type
of interview (e.g., telephone interview, personal interview, e-mail interview), and the date.

Carter, Luella. "Growing Georgia Greens." Personal interview.
5 Mar. 2008.

NOTE

See also "Interview, Published," page 176, and "Broadcast Interview,"
page 192.

Letter, Personal

Knight, Charles. Letter to the author. 21 Oct. 2008. MS.

Letter, Published

Eisenhower, Dwight. "Letter to Richard Nixon." 20 April 1968. *Memoirs of
Richard Nixon*. By Richard Nixon. New York: Grosset, 1978. Print.

Loose-Leaf Collections

If you cite an article from *SIRS, Opposing Viewpoints,* or other
loose-leaf collections, provide both the original publication data
and then add information for the loose-leaf volume, as shown in
this next example:

Teicher Khadaroo, Stacy. "Suicide Prevention Program Focuses on Teens."
Christian Science Monitor 3 Jan. 2008: n.p. Print. Boca Raton: SIRS,
2008. Art. 24.

Krasney, Ben. *City Crime Rankings: Crime in Metropolitan America*.
14th ed. *CQ Researcher* 18 Nov. 2007: 416. Washington, DC: CQ Press,
2007. Print.

Manuscript (MS) and Typescript (TS)

> Glass, Malcolm. Journal 3, MS. Malcolm Glass Private Papers, Clarksville, TN.
>
> Williams, Ralph. "Walking on the Water." 2009. TS.

Map

Treat a map as you would an anonymous work, but add a descriptive label, such as *map*, *chart*, or *survey*, unless the title describes the medium.

> *County Boundaries and Names.* United States Base Map GE-50, No. 86.
>
> Washington, DC: GPO, 2007. Print.
>
> *Pennsylvania.* Map. Chicago: Rand, 2008. Print.

Miscellaneous Materials (Program, Leaflet, Poster, Announcement)

> "Earth Day." Poster. Louisville. 20 Mar. 2008. Print.
>
> "Spring Family Weekend." Program. Nashville: Fisk U. 1 Apr. 2008. Print.

Musical Composition

For a musical composition, begin with the composer's name, followed by a period. Italicize the title of an opera, ballet, or work of music identified by name, but do not italicize or enclose within quotation marks the form, number, and key when these are used to identify an instrumental composition.

> Mozart, Wolfgang A. *Jupiter.* Symphony No. 41. London: n.p., 1999. CD.

Treat a published score as you would a book.

> Legrenzi, Giovanni. *La Buscha.* Sonata for Instruments. *Historical Anthology of*
>
> *Music.* Ed. Archibald T. Davison and Willi Apel. Cambridge, MA: Harvard
>
> UP, 1950. 70–76. Print.

Pamphlet

Treat a pamphlet as you would a book.

> Federal Reserve Board. *Consumer Handbook to Credit Protection Laws.*
>
> Washington, DC: GPO, 2007. Print.
>
> Westinghouse Advanced Power Systems. *Nuclear Waste Management:*
>
> *A Manageable Task.* Madison, PA: Author, n.d. Print.

Performance

Treat a performance (e.g., play, opera, ballet, or concert) as you would a film, but include the site (normally the theater and city) and the date of the performance.

Oklahoma Statehood: A Cherokee Perspective. Cherokee Heritage Center,
    Tahlequah, OK. 12 Apr. 2008. Performance.

Macbeth. By William Shakespeare. Folger Elizabethan Theatre, Washington,
    DC: 29 Mar. 2008. Performance.

If your text emphasizes the work of a particular individual, begin with
the appropriate name.

Szymanski, Natalie, Connie Sirois, Rachel Breneman, and Tom Thompson.
    "Developing Relevant and Responsible Writing Instruction." Conf. on Coll.
    Composition and Communication Convention. Hilton Riverside,
    New Orleans, 3 Apr. 2008. Address.

Ebersole, Christine, and Billy Stritch. "American Songbook." The Allen Room,
    New York. 29 Feb. 2008. Address.

Essman, Susie, comedian. Zanies, Chicago. 20 Mar. 2008. Address.

Public Address or Lecture

Identify the nature of the address (e.g., Lecture, Reading), include
the site (normally the lecture hall and city), and the date of the
performance.

Holl, Scott. "Taking Your Ancestors to Church: Finding Clues in
    Ecclesiastical Records." St. Louis Genealogical Soc., St. Louis.
    1 Mar. 2008. Address.

Recording on Record, Tape, or Disk

If you are not citing a compact disc, indicate the medium (e.g.,
audiocassette, audiotape [reel-to-reel tape], or LP [long-playing
record]).

"Chaucer: The Nun's Priest's Tale." *Canterbury Tales.* Narr. in Middle English by
    Alex Edmonds. London, 2005. Audiocassette.

Dylan, Bob. "The Times They Are A-Changin'." *Bob Dylan's Greatest Hits.* CBS,
    1967. CD.

Reich, Robert B. *Locked in the Cabinet: A Political Memoir.* 4 audiocassettes
    abridged. New York: Random Audio, 1997. Audiocassette.

Hancock, Herbie "Both Sides Now." *River: The Joni Letters.* n.p.: Verve,
    2007. CD.

Do not underscore, italicize, or enclose within quotation marks a
private recording or tape. However, you should include the date, if
available, as well as the location and the identifying number.

Drake, Marc. Early Settlers of the Smokey Mountains. Rec. Feb. 2007. U of
Knoxville. Knoxville, TN. UTF.34.82. Audiotape.

Cite a libretto, liner notes, or booklet that accompanies a recording in the form shown in the following example.

Crow, Sheryl. Booklet. *Detours*. By Sheryl Crow. A&M, 2008. Print.

Report

Unbound reports are placed within quotation marks; bound reports are treated as books.

McGruder Dynamics. *2008 Annual Report.* Atlanta: McGruder,
2008. Print.

Franco, Lynn. "Confidence Slips Amid Fragile Economy." The
Conference Board. New York: CBS/Broadcast Group, 23 Jan.
2006. Print.

Reproductions, Photographs, and Photocopies

Blake, William. *Comus*. Plate 4. "Blake's *Comus* Designs." *Blake Studies* 4
(Spring 1972): 61. Print.

Michener, James A. "Structure of Earth at Centennial, Colorado." Line
drawing in *Centennial*. By Michener. New York: Random, 1974.
26. Print.

Table, Illustration, Chart, or Graph

Tables or illustrations of any kind published within works need a detailed label (chart, table, figure, photograph, and so on).

"Communication Strategies Used by New Language Learners." Figure. *English
Journal* 97.3 (Jan. 2008): 23. Print.

Alphabet. Chart. Columbus, OH: Scholastic, 2008. Print.

Television or Radio Program

If available or relevant, provide information in this order: the episode (in quotation marks), the title of the program (italicized), title of the series (not italicized nor in quotation marks), name of the network, call letters and city of the local station, and the broadcast date. Add other information (such as narrator) after the episode or program narrated or directed or performed. Place the number of episodes, if relevant, before the title of the series.

"Border Security and Immigration Security." Host: Brian Lamb. *Washington Journal*. C-SPAN. 22 Feb 2006. Television.

"Elton John." *Larry King Live*. Host: Larry King. CNN. 25 Feb. 2008. Television.

Pride and Prejudice. By Jane Austin. 3 episodes. Masterpiece Theatre. Introd. Russell Baker. NPT, Nashville. 3 Feb. 2008. Television.

Thesis

See "Dissertation, Unpublished," page 193.

Transparency

Sharp, La Vaughn, and William E. Loeche. *The Patient and Circulatory Disorders: A Guide for Instructors.* 54 transparencies, 99 overlays. Philadelphia: Lorrenzo, 2005. Print.

Unpublished Paper

Schuler, Wren. "Prufrock and His Cat." Unpublished essay, 2008. Print.

CHAPTER 12

Creating Electronic Research Projects

This chapter suggests ways to create and publish your research project electronically. It begins with the easiest—putting a word-processed research paper on a disk for your instructor—and moves to the most difficult—designing a Web site and releasing the paper onto the Internet. This chapter will give you a sense of the possibilities of electronic research papers.

Creating your research paper electronically has a number of advantages:

- **It is easy.** Creating electronic research projects can be as simple as saving your paper in a computer file and publishing your paper electronically.

- **It offers multimedia potential.** Unlike paper documents, electronic documents enable you to include anything available in a digital form—including text, illustrations, sound, and video.

- **It can link your reader to more information.** Your readers can click a hyperlink to access additional sources of information. (A **hyperlink** or link is a highlighted word or image that, when clicked, lets readers jump from one place to another—for example, from your research paper to a Web site on your subject.)

12a Beginning the Electronic Project

Before you decide to create your research paper electronically, consider three questions to assist the development of the presentation:

1. **What support is provided by your school?** Most institutions have made investments in technology and the personnel to support it. Investigate how your college will help you publish in an electronic medium.

2. **Is electronic publishing suitable for your research topic?** Ask yourself what your readers will gain from reading an electronic text rather than the traditional paper version. Will an electronic format really help you get your ideas to readers?

3. **What form will it take?** Electronic research papers appear generally in one of the following forms:
   - A word-processed document (see section 12b)
   - An electronic slide show (see section 12c)
   - A Web site (see section 12d)

Each of these forms can be researched and produced using traditional methods, but the writing and presentation will differ.

12b Using Word Processing

The easiest way to create an electronic document is by using word processing programs such as Microsoft Word or Corel WordPerfect and then distributing your report in its electronic form rather than printing it out.

Most popular word processing programs include tools for handling features that will enhance your presentation:

- **Graphics.** Word processors can accommodate graphics in a variety of formats, including .gif and .jpg (see section 12f for more information on graphic formats).
- **Sound and video.** Word processors can include several common audio and video clip formats. Usually, the reader has to click on an icon to activate the clip.
- **Hyperlinks.** Readers can click to go to a Web site on the Internet for further reading.

There are unique advantages when using a word processor to create an electronic research paper. Using a word processor is familiar; you probably already use one to create your traditional research papers. It is also flexible; word processors give you more control over format and design.

However, using a word processor to create your electronic research paper has two disadvantages: The computer file created by your word processor can become quite large if you include graphics, sound, and video. Also, to view your paper, readers must own the same word-processing software and sometimes even the same version of the software. Nevertheless, a word processor works well in a classroom or computer laboratory that shares the same software.

12c Building Electronic Presentations

If you plan an oral presentation, an electronic slide show can help illustrate your ideas. Electronic presentations differ from word-processed documents in that each page, or slide, comprises one computer screen. By clicking, you can move to the next slide.

The most common programs for creating electronic presentations are Microsoft PowerPoint and Corel Presentations. Both help you create a series of slides for presentation on your computer screen or through a projector to a large screen. These programs allow you to include graphics, sound, and other elements. More complex, standalone presentations with multimedia animation—designed for distribution on CD-ROM or through the Internet—can be created with programs such as Macromedia Director and Hyperstudio.

For small audiences you can usually present the show on a computer screen. For larger audiences, you may need a wide-screen television or a data projector. Check with your instructor or school technology specialist to find out what presentation equipment is available.

As you create your electronic presentation, consider the following suggestions:

- Because each slide can hold only limited information, condense the content of each slide to key points and fill in the details orally.
- Use the slide show to support your oral presentation.
- If appropriate, include graphics from your research project in your slide show.
- End the slide show with a carefully designed closing slide or an empty slide so that people will know the presentation is finished.

If you distribute the slide show by disk, CD, or the Web, you will probably need to adjust the presentation by adding more information to the slides because your oral commentary will be unavailable to the viewer—or you can record your audio commentary for inclusion with the presentation.

12d Research Paper Web Pages and Sites

A Web site can be an exciting and flexible way to convey your research. It is also the easiest way to get your work out to a large audience. Like an electronic presentation, a research paper Web site can include graphics, sound, and video.

Creating a Web page or a Web site involves collecting or making a series of computer files—some that contain the basic text and layout for your pages, and others that contain the graphics, sounds, or video that goes in your pages. These files are assembled together automatically when you view them in a Web browser.

> **NOTE**
>
> For more information on building Web pages and sites, see the "Beginner's Guide to HTML" at http://www.cs.trinity.edu/About/ The_Courses/cs301/html/HTMLPrimerAll.html or http://www.kean .edu/HomePages/beginnersGuide.htm.

Creating a Single Web Page

If you want to create a single Web page from your research paper, the easiest but most limited method is to save your word-processed research paper in HTML (Hyper Text Markup Language, the computer language that controls what Web sites look like). Different word-processing programs perform this process differently; so consult your software's help menu for specific instructions.

When the word-processing software converts your document to HTML, it also converts any graphics you have included to separate graphics files. Together, your text and the graphics can be viewed in a Web browser like any other Web page.

Your research paper will look somewhat different in HTML format than in its word-processed format. In some ways, HTML is less flexible than word processing, but you can still use word-processing software to make changes to your new HTML-formatted paper.

> **NOTE**
>
> The reader will need to scroll down the screen to continue to read the document.

Creating a Web Site with Multiple Pages

A multiple-page Web site allows you to assemble a large number of shorter pages, which are easy for readers to access and read. It requires careful planning and organization.

Creating a multipage Web site means creating one Web page after another—you repeat the basic process to create each page, and you add links between pages so readers can navigate easily from one to the next. Start with a home page that includes a title, a basic description of your project, and an index with hyperlinks to the contents of your site. Navigational elements, like links to the home page and other major pages of your site, provide a way for readers to "turn the pages" of your report.

Using an Editor to Create Web Pages

The easiest way to create your pages is with a Web page editor such as Microsoft FrontPage, Adobe Page Mill, or Netscape Composer. These programs work differently, but they all do the same thing—create Web pages. Using them is like using a word processor: You enter or paste in text, insert graphics or other multimedia objects, and save the file.

Importing, Entering, and Modifying Text

You can create your text within the Web page editor or outside it. To import text, simply copy it from your word processor and paste it into your Web page editor. You can also specify fonts, font sizes, font styles (such as bold), alignment, lists with bullets, and numbered lists. Here are a few tips for entering text into a Web page:

- **Use bold rather than underlining for emphasis and titles.** On a Web site, links are often underlined, so any other underlining can cause confusion.
- **Do not use tabs.** HTML does not support tabs for indenting the first line of a paragraph. You also will not be able to use hanging indents for your bibliography.

■ **Do not double-space.** The Web page editor automatically single spaces lines of text and double-spaces between paragraphs.

■ **Make all lines flush left** on the Works Cited page; HTML does not support the hanging indentions.

Citing Your Sources in a Web Research Paper

If you are using MLA, APA, or CSE styles, include parenthetical citations in the text itself and create a separate Web page for references. Remember to include such a page in your plans. Do not put footnotes at the bottom of each of your Web pages. Instead, use endnotes and create a separate page that holds all of the notes, just as you would have a separate page for the Works Cited or References pages. Create each note number in the text as a link to the notes page so readers can click on the number to go to the note. Remember to have a link on the notes page or Works Cited page to take the reader back again to the text.

12e Planning Electronic Research Papers

Because creating an electronic research paper can be more complicated than creating a traditional paper, it's important to plan your project carefully.

Creating a Plan for Your Research Paper

The following questions will help you think through the planning of your project.

■ **Assignment.** Does your instructor have specific requirements for this assignment you should keep in mind?

■ **Project description.** What topic will you be writing on?

■ **Purpose.** What are your reasons for creating an electronic project? Are you going to blend photographs of the 1960s with an essay on the civil rights movement? Or provide audio examples in an essay on John F. Kennedy's speeches?

■ **Audience.** Are you writing for the instructor, or will there be a broader audience, such as classmates or readers on the Web?

■ **Format.** Will your research paper be a word-processed document, an electronic presentation, or a Web site?

■ **Multimedia content.** What information, other than text, will you present? Do you have the tools available to scan or import multimedia?

■ **Structure.** How will you organize your document?

Designing Your Electronic Research Paper

Reading any kind of electronic document can be difficult for the reader unless you take special care in designing it. Aim for the following:

- **A consistent look and feel.** Make your research paper look very consistent throughout. Presentation software usually includes ready-made templates that help you to create a consistent look and feel.
- **A subtle design.** It is easy to create a Web site or presentation that includes all the bells and whistles—but such documents are hard to navigate and even harder to read. Avoid distractions like blinking text, garish colors, or unnecessary animations.
- **Ease of navigation.** Include consistent navigation tools so readers can see where they are and where they can go next.
- **Legibility.** Because readers often access electronic documents through a computer screen, legibility is important. Make the contrast between your text and background colors strong enough that readers can see the text easily. Avoid using the italic fonts, which are difficult to see on a computer screen.

> **NOTE**
>
> For more information on Web site design, see the "Yale C/AIM WWW Style Guide" at http://www.webstyleguide.com/index.html?/.

12f Using Graphics in Your Electronic Research Paper

Graphics will give your electronic text some exciting features that are usually foreign to the traditional research paper. They go beyond words on a printed page to pictures, sound, video clips, animation, and a vivid use of full-color art.

Decorative graphics make the document look more attractive but seldom add to the paper's content. Most clip art, for example, is decorative.

Illustration graphics provide a visual amplification of the text. For example, a picture of Thomas Hardy would reinforce and augment a research paper on the British poet and novelist.

Information graphics, such as charts, graphs, or tables, provide data about your topic.

Graphic File Formats

Graphics usually take up a lot of space, but you can save them as either JPEG or GIF files to make them smaller. In fact, Web sites can use graphics saved in these formats only. Both formats compress redundant information in a file, making it smaller while retaining most of the image quality. You can recognize the file format by looking at the extension to the file name—GIFs have the extension .gif, and JPEGs have the extension .jpg or .jpeg. GIF stands for Graphical Interchange Format, which develops and transfers digital images. JPEG stands for Joint Photographic Experts Group, which compresses color images to smaller files for ease of transport.

> **NOTE**
>
> For more information on JPEG and GIF files, go to one of these sites: Wide Area Communications at http://www.widearea.co.uk/designer/compress.html or Graphics 101 at About.com, at http://graphicdesign.about.com/.

In general, JPEGs work best for photographs and GIFs work best for line drawings. To save a file as a GIF or JPEG, open it in an image-editing program like Adobe Photoshop and save the file as one of the two types (for example, thardy.jpg or thardy.gif).

When the graphic is ready, you can insert it into your electronic research paper. Programs usually have specific menu commands for inserting graphics; refer to your user documentation to find out how to do so.

You can also borrow images from clip art or other Web sites (with proper documentation, of course). To borrow an image, go to the site with your Web browser, right-click on the image that you want, and left-click on "Save image as . . ." to put it on your hard drive or a portable storage device. You can then insert the image into your research paper.

> **NOTE**
>
> For more information on securing permission for borrowed material on your Web site, see Chapter 5, pages 68–69.

Creating Your Own Digital Graphics

Making your own graphics file is complex but rewarding. It adds a personal creativity to your research paper. Use one of the following techniques:

- **Use a graphics program,** such as Macromedia Freehand or Adobe Illustrator. With such software you can create a graphic file and save it as a JPEG or GIF file.
- **Use a scanner** to copy your drawings, graphs, photographs, and other matter. Programs such as Adobe Photoshop and JASC Paintshop Pro are useful for modifying scanned photographs.
- **Create original photographs with a digital camera.** Digital cameras usually save images as JPEGs, so you will not need to convert the files into a usable format.

As long as you create JPEG files or GIF files for your graphics, you can transport the entire research paper to a Web site.

12g Using Sound and Video in Your Electronic Research Paper

Because it usually requires additional hardware and software, working with sound and video can be complicated. It also makes your research paper large and difficult to compress and transfer. Before attempting to use digital audio or video, check into your own resources as well as those of your instructor and school. Many institutions have invested heavily in multimedia technology, while others have not.

A detailed discussion of digital audio and video is beyond the scope of this chapter, but the Web holds a wealth of information on the subject.

NOTE

For information on digital audio and video, consult the following Web site: Webmonkey's multimedia tutorial for audio and video resources, at http://www.webmonkey.com/multimedia/.

12h Delivering Your Electronic Research Paper to Readers

Follow your instructor's requirements for delivering your electronic research paper or use one of the techniques in the following checklist.

☐ **Zip disk.** A Zip disk or other proprietary format will hold much larger files, but your reader/professor must own a drive that can read it.

☐ **CD-ROM disc.** These discs hold large amounts of data and thus work well for transmitting graphics, sound, or video files. However, you must own or have access to a CD-R (Compact Disk Recordable) or CD-RW (Compact Disk Recordable/Writeable) drive. Most readers will have regular CD-ROM drives that can read your discs, but you might want to confirm this beforehand.

☐ **High-speed USB flash drive.** These devices hold large amounts of data, so they work well for transmitting graphics, sound, or video files. Their compact size and plug-and-play operation allow your instructor to easily view content on a laptop or desktop computer with a USB port.

☐ **E-mail.** E-mailing your file as an attachment is the fastest way to deliver your electronic research paper; however, it works best if you have a single file, like a word-processed research paper, rather than a collection of related files, like a Web site.

☐ **Web site.** If you have created a Web site or Web page, you can upload your work to a Web server and readers can access your work on the Internet. Procedures for uploading Web sites vary from school to school and server to server; work closely with your instructor and Webmaster to perform this process successfully. Regardless of what method you choose, be sure to follow your instructor's directions and requirements.

12i Preparing a Writing Portfolio

Writing is a form of art, but unlike other art forms such as dance or sculpture, writers usually do not invite others to watch them perform. Instead, it is the finished product that can have the most influence on others and also demonstrates a writer's abilities. But how can a writer, especially a student writer, demonstrate his or her writing ability to their peers, professors, the public, or more importantly, to a potential employer? The answer is a writing portfolio.

Over the past decade, writing portfolios have become a choice assessment tool for many instructors. As a result, most students who have participated in writing projects, from high school to PhD programs, have assembled portfolios of some kind. Writing portfolios provide a tangible demonstration of talent and experience. Your portfolio will include selected previous written works in a class, plus any additional assignments that the instructor requests. The Writing portfolio has several benefits:

- It provides clear objectives and evaluative criteria for writing assignments.
- It provides a real audience as you learn to direct your writing to an unknown reader.
- It provides informed feedback from your instructor, peers, and writing associates.

Specifically, the writing portfolio is a purposeful collection of writing assembled to demonstrate specified writing capabilities to an audience. Usually, a portfolio is used to demonstrate writing skills and talents, but it can also be used for obtaining a job, documenting job performance, or gaining entrance into an educational institution. In some respects, the writing portfolio is an individual's creative resume. Although it is not an actual resume, the writing portfolio displays the works and documents that a resume mentions. In that sense, the collection of writings gives a three-dimensional or amplified view of a learner's abilities.

At first, selecting folio material may seem like an overwhelming task, especially if you are starting from scratch. The truth is that most writers have many writing samples available. Listed here are some potential places to begin looking for folio material:

- Coursework from your classes, not just writing courses. Hanging on to class notebooks and assignments is beneficial and provides writing examples from a number of subject areas.
- Previous essays and research projects. These are great because they usually contain the writer's "best" work and include self-analysis essays regarding strengths and weaknesses as a writer.
- Journals and personal writing. Unconstrained writing reveals a lot about a writer's style and preferred voice.

Although the portfolio philosophy is to save everything, you need not feel pressured to hoard every scrap of writing. Instead, a light screening of portfolio materials should be conducted to prevent an unmanageable collection of samples from forming. Use the following criteria to help select folio material:

- Select materials that clearly demonstrate your abilities.
- Select materials based on quality. Choose documents that demonstrate audience analysis, grammar, clarity, conciseness, technical information, instructions, page layout and design, organization, group or independent work, diversity, and variety.

- Select materials that demonstrate learning. For instance, if a particular piece demonstrates your understanding of persuasive methods, include it.
- Select materials that will have long-term value and usefulness.

Storing and organizing the portfolio material can be chaotic. There are many storage/organizing products available. For example, expandable folders work nicely for grouping material because they come in varying sizes and can accommodate odd-sized documents. Another organizing option is a three-ring binder. If you use a three-ring binder, consider using plastic sheet protectors to store pages; it is better to avoid punching holes in your work if possible. Some people keep folio materials in a file drawer and organize the materials in files. You could also use a plastic storage container. Keeping your work on a USB flash drive is another option. Choose whatever works best for you, but be sure to put the folio collection somewhere where it will be safe from damage or loss.

> **NOTE**
>
> The safest and most dependable way to store your materials is both in hard copy and on a flash drive.

Begin creating a collection of any and all materials that you might want to place in your writing portfolio. Remember, the portfolio philosophy is SAVE EVERYTHING! The more material you collect in your portfolio, the broader the selection and greater the flexibility you will have when pulling together a presentation of your writing talents.

> **NOTE**
>
> For information on preparing a writing portfolio, consult the following Web site: http://writing.colostate.edu/guides/teaching/co301aman/pop5a.cfm.

12j Presenting Research in Alternative Formats

Current technology provides various options for presenting your research project. Desktop publishing programs such as Microsoft

Publisher, Adobe PageMaker, or Broderbund Print Shop provide templates for the effective design of newsletters and brochures. Consider an alternative format for your findings when it includes information that can inform or assist a broad array of readers.

Often printed on both sides of a sheet of paper, **newsletters** usually contain multiple pages. **Brochures** are formatted with columns or "panels" that are designed to fit on the front and back of one single sheet of paper so that it can easily be folded. Both newsletters and brochures follow certain conventions of style:

- Place your information in a logical order.
- Use a type size, font style, and color of text that is easy to read.
- Use left-justified formatting that leaves a "ragged" right-hand margin. This is a style that is easier for readers to follow.
- Avoid distracting gaps between words and awkward hyphens dividing words at the end of lines.
- Keep paragraphs short when information is presented in columns.

For most class projects, newsletters and brochures can be printed from your personal computer. For documents in the workplace or for a social group, you may choose to consider using a professional printer; however, remember that a print agency will charge for its services.

Alternative formats for the presentation of your research, such as newsletters and brochures, should stimulate interest and highlight the key components of the project.

CHECKLIST: Publishing Alternative Documents

☐ Decide on the purpose of the document and the response that you want the audience to have about the information.

☐ Sketch out or visualize how each section or panel will look.

☐ Select a paper size, binding, or folding that presents your research in a straightforward, clear method.

☐ Consider graphics, colors, and formatting that add to the clarity of your document.

☐ Use a distinctive font in the masthead or title as well as headlines for the sections of the document that emphasize their importance.

☐ Make each section or panel an independent item that can be understood if the brochure is folded or turned to a secondary page.

☐ Limit information to what readers can comprehend in a brief reading, while informing them where more information can be found.

Your Research Project

1. If you are interested in producing an electronic research paper, consult with your instructor for advice and to learn about institutional support.
2. Begin by building a basic model with word processing, one that might include graphics and other elements as described in section 12f.
3. If the assignment includes an oral presentation, consider building a slide show as described in section 12c.
4. Try building a Web page and then a Web site. Consult with your instructor before uploading it to the Web.
5. Make yourself comfortable about your knowledge of technical terms such as Zip disk, CD-ROM, USB flash drive, e-mail, and Web site.

Sample Research Paper

Formatting the Paper in MLA Style

The format of a research paper consists of the following parts. It is essential that you have a title, body of the paper, and a Works Cited page.

1. Title page or opening page with title
2. Outline
3. The text of the paper
4. Content notes
5. Appendix
6. Works Cited

Title Page or Opening Page

A research paper in MLA style does not need a separate title page unless you include an outline, abstract, or other introductory matter. See page 215 for an example.

Outline

Include your outline with the finished manuscript only if your instructor requires it.

The Text of the Paper

Double-space your entire paper. In general, you should not use subtitles or numbered divisions for your paper, even if it becomes twenty pages long. Do not start "Notes" or "Works Cited" on the final page of text.

Content Endnotes Page

Label this page with the word "Notes" centered at the top edge of the sheet, at least one double-space below your page numbering sequence in the upper-right corner. Double-space between the "Notes" heading and the first note. Number the notes in sequence with raised superscript numerals to match those within your text. Double-space all entries and double-space between them.

Appendix

Place additional material, if necessary, in an appendix that precedes the Works Cited page. This is the logical location for tables and illustrations, computer data, questionnaire results, complicated statistics, mathematical proofs, or detailed descriptions of special equipment.

Works Cited

Center the heading "Works Cited" one inch from the top edge of the sheet. Continue the page numbering sequence in the upper-right corner. Double-space throughout. Use hanging indention—that is, set the first line of each entry flush left and indent subsequent lines five spaces or one-half inch. Alphabetize by the last name of the author. See page 219 for an example.

Writing a Literary Paper in MLA Style

Sample Research Paper

The sample research paper demonstrates the form and style of a literary research paper written to the specifications of the MLA style. Annotations in the margins explain elements of style that may be important in the development of your paper.

Anthony Murphy

English 1102

Dr. Pasch

November 1, 2009

Wilfred Owen—Battlefront Poet

Murphy opens with background information.

    In the summer of 1917, World War I was at its peak.
Countries were being torn apart, men were being slaughtered
by the thousands, and the civilians were starving. But out of
the mists of this carnage came one of the greatest war poets
of the twentieth century. With his horrific imagery, and
antiwar themes, Owen shows readers the darker side of

Murphy establishes the concept he will explore.

war. Although his life was cut short, the poems of Wilfred
Owen describes for readers around the world the
consequences of war.

    Born in March 1893 in a house near Oswestry, England,
Wilfred Owen spent most of his childhood reading the
scriptures and learning the ways of the church. As a
committed Christian and with a "pious mother . . .
[urging] him to become an Anglican priest," according to Rich
Geib, Owen seriously considered entering the ministry. Instead
he decided to attend the University of London, where
unfortunately he was denied a scholarship and therefore had
to work as a reverend's liaison to pay his tuition. By the age
of nineteen, Owen had already immersed himself in poetry,
being especially impressed with Keats and Shelley (Roberts).
After a few years of college, he made his way to Bordeaux,
France, to work as a private tutor at the Berlitz School. It was
here that Owen first received word that war had broken out
between the European nations.

    During the first year of the war, Owen frequently visited
soldiers who had been wounded during battle. After being
influenced by what he saw in the hospitals and national
propaganda encouraging young men to enlist, Owen decided
to join the military (Roberts; Geib). In the fall of 1915, Owen

Murphy cites the authorities on Owen in brief but effective ways.

left France and headed to England to enlist in the Army. In June he became a second lieutenant and made a brief statement at his commissioning: "I came out in order to help these boys—directly by leading them as well as an officer can" (qtd. in Geib). After Owen's commission, he was given a platoon under the Manchester division, which was sent to the trenches of France in January 1917. It was these first days of battle "where his outlook on life changed permanently" (Geib). For months he dodged bullets and bombs only to see his men be killed daily. In April, Owen's luck ran out, and his trench was hit with a stream of explosions. Suffering from shell shock, he was evacuated to Craiglockhart War Hospital. It was here that Owen would meet the inspiration to his destiny.

Siegfried Sassoon was already an acclaimed poet when Owen met him. Sassoon became a mentor to Owen and introduced him to renowned poets Robert Graves and H. G. Wells ("Wilfred Owen"). Sassoon also helped Owen in his writing of the poems "Anthem for Doomed Youth" and "Dulce et Decorum Est." With Sassoon's assistance, Owen spent the next several months developing and writing his poetry. In June 1918, Owen was sent back to the lines to join his regiment, but not before completing numerous poems. As noted by Dr. Stuart Lee, it was here at Craiglockhart where "[Owen] wrote many of the poems for which he is remembered today."

Owen rejoined the 2nd Manchester Regiment in Scarborough, and was immediately sent back to France. In October, as the Great War was coming to an end, Owen's unit was still on the offensive. As Owen's men entered the town of Amien, they were attacked by a German machine gun. Owen advanced the German position and defeated the enemy single-handedly. Due to his heroic acts, he was awarded the Military Cross for Bravery ("Multimedia"). On November 11, 1918, the Armistice was signed and World War I had officially ended. People all over the world were cheering and celebrating, including the parents of Wilfred Owen. But on the afternoon of that day, Owen's parents received a telegram informing them that their son had been killed just seven days prior.

"It was only when the war and his life came to an end that his poetry was truly recognized" ("Examine"). After two years, Owen's poems were finally published, thanks to the work of his mentor Siegfried Sassoon. In December 1920, Sassoon published a book called *Poems of Wilfred Owen* that consisted of ten of Owen's best poems, with each poem introduced by Sassoon. One poem that was not put into the book was "Disabled." "'Disabled' presents a poignant picture of a young soldier 'legless, sewn short at elbow '. . . and shows what he had been before against what he is left with," writes Kenneth Simcox of the Wilfred Owen Association.

Lines of the poem are identified, line breaks are maintained, and the line numbers are listed.

> He sat in a wheeled chair, waiting for dark,
> And shivered in his ghastly suit of grey,
> Legless, sewn short at elbow. Through the park
> Voices of boys rang saddening like a hymn,
> Voices of play and pleasure after day,
> Till gathering sleep had mothered them from
> him. (l.1–5)

This section demonstrates the manner in which Murphy interprets one of the poems, citing from it and explaining the implications in light of the poetic theme.

"Disabled" is a perfect example of Owen's antiwar feelings. There is a sense of negativity just from the title alone (Groves). The character in the story is never given a name, which adds a feeling of worthlessness to his life ("Examine"). The poem further relates how the soldier only went to war to impress the girls, and now all people do is pity him rather than thank him. The soldier never really wanted to go to war, but pressure led him to do so. Paul Groves describes the pressure by stating, "The soldier was already a football hero . . . and now the soldier must become a war hero as well." The poem was written not only to have pity for these soldiers but to reflect the personal conflict Owen had with his enlistment. "Disabled" shows that people have different reasons for going to war and illustrates the effects that war has on men, both mentally and physically (Groves). The overall message of "Disabled," however, is do not let others dictate your life.

With the signing of the Armistice, peace was finally realized for a brief period of time. Wilfred Owen opened the minds of many readers after the war by showing that soldiers just do not always sign up willingly and that battle during or after war is never glorious. Although he is gone, Wilfred Owen's life lives on through the poems he left the world—"My subject is War, and the pity of War. The Poetry is in the pity" (qtd. Geib).

Works Cited

Bradbury, Malcolm, ed. *The Atlas of Literature*. New York: Stewart, Tabori, & Chang, 1998. Print.

"Examine the Way Three Poems by Wilfred Owen Depict the Horror of War." Coursework Help. 2008. Web. 25 Oct. 2006.

Geib, Rich. "Wilfred Owen: Poet, Patriot, Soldier, Pacifist." Rich Geib's Universe. 1 Oct. 2006. Web. 16 Oct. 2006.

Groves, Paul. "Wilfred Owen." 25 July 2005. Web. 16 Oct. 2009.

Lee, Stuart. "Wilfred Owen." Wilfred Owen Multimedia Digital Archive. 22 July 2005. Web. 29 Oct. 2006.

Lusty, Heather. "Shaping the National Voice: Poetry of WWI." *Journal of Modern Literature*. 30.1 (Fall 2006): 199–209. Print.

"Multimedia and Document Library." *LiterActive*. CD-ROM. Boston: Bedford, St. Martins. 2006.

Norris, Margot. "Teaching World War I Poetry—Comparatively." *College Literature*. 32.3 (Summer 2005): 136–153. Print.

Roberts, David. "Wilfred Owen: Greatest War Poet in the English Language." 1999. Web. 18 Oct. 2006.

Simcox, Kenneth. "Disabled." Wilfred Owen Association. 2001. Web. 29 Oct. 2006.

"Wilfred Owen." Academy of American Poets. 1997. Web. 18 Oct. 2006.

Glossary of Manuscript Style

The alphabetical glossary that follows will answer most of your miscellaneous questions about matters of form, such as margins, pagination, dates, and numbers. For matters not addressed below, consult the index, which will direct you to appropriate pages elsewhere in this text.

Abbreviations

Employ abbreviations often and consistently in notes and citations, but avoid them in the text. In your citations, but not in your text, always abbreviate these items:

- Technical terms and reference words (anon., e.g., diss.)
- Institutions (acad., assn., Cong.)
- Dates (Jan., Feb.)
- States and countries (OH, CA, USA)
- Names of publishers (McGraw, UP of Florida)
- Titles of literary works (*Ado* for *Much Ado About Nothing*)
- Books of the Bible (Exod. for Exodus)

Accent Marks

When you quote, reproduce accents exactly as they appear in the original.

"La tradición clásica en españa," according to Romana, remains strong in public school instruction (16).

Ampersand

Avoid using the ampersand symbol "&" unless custom demands it, as in the John Updike story title "A & P."

Arabic Numerals

Arabic numerals should be used whenever possible: for volumes, books, parts, and chapters of works; acts, scenes, and lines of plays; cantos, stanzas, and lines of poetry.

Figures and Tables

A table is a systematic presentation of materials, usually in columns. A figure is any nontext item that is not a table: blueprint, chart, diagram, drawing, graph, photo, photostat, map, and so on. Use graphs appropriately. A line graph serves a different purpose than a circle (pie) chart, and a bar graph plots different information than a scatter graph. Place captions above a table and below a figure. Here is an example:

Table 1
Response by Class on Nuclear Energy Policy

	Freshman	Sophomore	Junior	Senior
1. More nuclear power	150	301	75	120
2. Less nuclear power	195	137	111	203
3. Present policy is acceptable	87	104	229	31

Foreign Cities

In general, spell the names of foreign cities as they are written in original sources. However, for purposes of clarity, you may substitute an English name or provide both with one in parentheses:

Köln (Cologne)   Braunschweig (Brunswick)

Indention

Indent first lines of paragraphs five spaces or a half-inch. Indent all lines of long quotations (four lines or more) ten spaces or one inch from the left margin.

Italics

Use *italics* in place of underscoring for titles and words that require emphasis.

Margins

A basic one-inch margin on all sides is recommended. Place your page number one-half inch down from the top edge of the paper and one inch from the right edge. Your software will provide a ruler, menu, or style palette that allows you to set the margins. *Note:* If you develop a header, the running head may appear one inch from the top, in which case your first line of text will begin 1-1/2 inches from the top.

Names of Persons

As a general rule, the first mention of a person requires the full name (e.g., Ernest Hemingway or Margaret Mead) and thereafter give only the surname (e.g., Hemingway or Mead). *Note:* APA style uses last name only in the text. Omit formal titles (Mr., Mrs., Dr., Hon.) in textual and note references to distinguished persons, living or dead.

Numbering Pages

Use a running head to number your pages in the upper right-hand corner of the page. Depending on the software, you can create the head with the "numbering" or the "header" feature. See the sample paper for page numbers in MLA style, pages 215–219.

Roman Numerals

Use capital Roman numerals for titles of persons (Elizabeth II) and major sections of an outline (see pages 89–90). Use lowercase Roman numerals for preliminary pages of text, as for a preface or introduction (iii, iv, v). Otherwise, use Arabic numerals (e.g., Vol. 5, Act 2, Ch. 17, Plate 21, 2 Sam. 2.1–8, or *Iliad* 2.121–30), *except* when writing for some instructors in history, philosophy, religion, music, art, and theater, in which case you may need to use Roman numerals (e.g., III, Act II, I Sam. ii.1–8, *Hamlet* I.ii.5–6).

Running Heads

Repeat your last name in the upper right corner of every page just in front of the page number (see the sample paper, pages 215–219).

Proofreading Marks

Be familiar with the most common proofreading symbols so that you can correct your own copy or mark your copy for a typist. Some of the most common proofreading symbols are shown on page 224.

Shortened Titles in the Text

Use abbreviated titles of books and articles mentioned often in the text after a first, full reference. For example, after initial usage, *Backgrounds to English as Language* should be shortened to *Backgrounds* in the text, notes, and in-text citations.

Spacing

As a general rule, double-space everything—the body of the paper, all indented (block) quotations, and all reference entries. Footnotes, if used, should be single-spaced, but endnotes should be double-spaced.

Titles within Titles

For a title to a book that includes another title indicated by quotation marks, retain the quotation marks.

O. Henry's Irony in "The Gift of the Magi"

Common Proofreading Symbols

ι	error in spelling (m*i*stake) with correction in margin
lc	lowercase (mis*t*ake)
⌒	close up (mis take)
I	delete and close up (miss take)
⊢─⊣	delete and close up more than one letter (the mistakes and errors continue)
∧	insert (mi~s~take)
∿	transpose elements (th*ei*f)
⬭	material to be corrected or moved, with instructions in the margin, or material to be spelled out ((corp.))
caps or ≡	capitalize (Huck finn and Tom Sawyer)
¶	begin a paragraph
No¶	do not begin a paragraph
∧	insert
e	delete (a mistakes)
#	add space
⊙	add a period
⌃	add a comma
⌃	add a semicolon
∨	add an apostrophe or single closing quotation mark
∨	add a single opening quotation mark
∨ ∨	add double quotation marks
bf	change to boldface
ital	change to italic
stet	let stand as it is; ignore marks
¢/ǂ or ( )	add parentheses
=	add a hyphen

For a title of an article within quotation marks that includes a title to a book, as indicated by underlining, retain the underlining or use italics.

"Great Expectations as a Novel of Initiation"

"*Great Expectations* as a Novel of Initiation"

For a title of an article within quotation marks that includes another title indicated by quotation marks, enclose the shorter title within single quotation marks.

"A Reading of O. Henry's 'The Gift of the Magi'"

For an underscored title to a book that incorporates another title that normally receives underscoring, do not underscore or italicize the shorter title nor place it within quotation marks.

Interpretations of Great Expectations

<u>Using Shakespeare's</u> Romeo and Juliet <u>in the Classroom</u>

Underscoring (*Italicizing*)

Do not underscore sacred writings (Genesis or Old Testament); series (The New American Nation Series); editions (Variorum Edition of W. B. Yeats); societies (Victorian Society); courses (Greek Mythology); divisions of a work (preface, appendix, canto 3, scene 2); or descriptive phrases (Nixon's farewell address or Reagan's White House years).

Underscoring Individual Words for Emphasis

Italicizing words for emphasis is discouraged. A better alternative is to position the keyword in such a way as to accomplish the same purpose. For example:

EXPRESSED EMPHASIS: Perhaps an answer lies in <u>preventing</u> abuse, not in makeshift remedies after the fact.

BETTER: Prevention of abuse is a better answer than makeshift remedies after the fact.

Some special words and symbols require italics or underlining.

- Species, genera, and varieties:

Penstemon caespitosus subsp. *thompsoniae*

- Letter, word, or phrase cited as a linguistic sample:

  the letter <u>e</u> in the word <u>let</u>

- Letters used as statistical symbols and algebraic variables:

  trial <u>n</u> of the <u>t</u> test or <u>C</u>(3, 14) = 9.432

Word Division

Avoid dividing any word at the end of a line. Leave the line short rather than divide a word.

credits

Chapter 2

Figure 2.1, p. 27: Entry "Differentiated Instruction" from *Bibliographic Index,* 2005. Copyright © 2005 by The H.W. Wilson Company. Reprinted by permission.

Figure 2.2, p. 30: Entry for "Antidepressants" from *Readers' Guide to Periodic Literature,* 2006. Reprinted by permission of the H.W. Wilson Company. Copyright © 2006. Material reproduced with permission of the publisher.

Figure 2.3, p. 33: From "Lawmaker: Home-Schoolers Shouldn't Have Tougher ACT Mark," by Duren Cheek, *The Tennessean,* October 23, 2003. Copyright © 2003 by *The Tennessean.* Reprinted by permission.

Chapter 10

p. 134: From "Parenthood" by Karen S. Peterson, *USA Today,* September 19, 1990.

Figure 10.1, p. 134: Reprinted by permission of the Modern Language Association of America from H. R. Walley's "Shakespeare's Conception of Hamlet," *PMLA* (1933): pp. 777–9 (sample pages from JSTOR database).

p. 137: "The Red Wheelbarrow" by William Carlos Williams from *Collected Poems: 1909–1939, Volume 1.* Copyright 1938 by New Directions Publishing Corp. Reprinted by permission of New Directions Publishing Corporation and Carcanet Press Limited.

p. 146: First three lines from "Morning Song" from *Ariel* by Sylvia Plath. Copyright © 1961 by Ted Hughes. Reprinted by permission of HarperCollins Publishers Inc. and by Faber and Faber Ltd.

index

P

Page number in citations, 128–130
Page references, 128–130
Pagination, 222
Painting, online, citation, 187
Pamphlet files, 34
  citation, 195
Paradigms, *see* academic models, **79–88**
Paraphrase notes, 95–96
Parenthesis, 128–130, 151–152
Parenthetical Citations, **128–153**
Passive voice, 119
Past tense, 118–119
Peer review, 126
Performance, academic model, 82
Performance, citation, 195
Period, 140–141
Periodicals. *See also* Journals; Magazines; Newspapers
  citation of, **174–179**
  indexes, 29–32
  online, citation of, 184
Personal ideas, as source of topics, 3
Personal interview, 6
Personal notes, 92–93
Personal papers, gathering data from, 56
Personal web site, citation, 186
Persuasion, 15
  academic pattern, 83–84, 113
Philosophy
  academic model, 81–82
  search engines, 41
Photo, online, citation, 187
Photocopies, citation, 197
Photograph, citation, 197
Physical sciences,
  academic style, 112–113
  database search, 26
  field research, 53
  indexes, 31
  source materials for, 72
Place of publication, 161–162
Plagiarism, **62–69**
  avoiding, 65–68
  bias in a source, 63–64
  collaborative projects, 68
  common knowledge exceptions to, 66–67
  credibility, 62–63
  documenting sources, 66
  honoring property rights, 64–65

identifying bias, 63–64
publishing on a Web site, 68–69
source credibility, 62–63
Plays & drama, citation, 170
  quoting, 147
Plot summary note, 97–98
Poem, online, citation, 187
Poetry, citation of, 144–147, 170
Political science search engines, 43
Portfolio writing, 208–210
Poster, citation, 197
Preface, citation, 169
Preliminary outline, 3
Present perfect tense, 117
Present tense, 118
Primary sources, 71–72, 94
Printed bibliographies, searching, 27–29
Printed materials
  as source of topics, 7–8
  bibliography search, 27–29
  biography search, 32–33
  government documents, 34–35
  index search, 29–32
  newspaper search, 33–34
  pamphlet files, 34
Printed source, citation, 225
Problem, in thesis, 122
Program, citation, 197
Proofreading, 126–127
  marks and symbols, 223–224
Property rights, honoring, 64–65
Pseudonym, author, 163
Psychology database search, 24–25
  search engines, 43
Public address, citation, 56, 196
  gathering data from, 56
Public statute, citation, 182
Publication information, 161
Publication on personal websites, 202–204
Publishing and fair rights, 68–69
Punctuation of citations, 140–143
Purpose statement, 15

Q

Qualification statement, 16
Qualitative methodologies, 58–59

Quantitative methodologies, 58–59
Queries, citation, 177
Question marks, 142–143
Questionnaires
  gathering data from, 58–59, 98
Questions, to refine a topic, 4–5
Quotation notes, 93–95
Quotations, in-text citations, 143
  altering initial capital letters, 147–148
  brackets, 151–152
  ellipsis points in, 148–151
  indentation of, 142–147
  omitted material, 148–151
  parenthesis, 151–152
  parentheses and brackets in, 151–152
  of a play, 147
  of poetry, 144–147
  primary sources, 94
  secondary sources, 94–95
  translations, 146–147

R

Racial identity, terminology used to describe, 121
Radio programs, citation, 188
Rationale for the project, 15
Recording, citation, 188
Reading Personal Papers, gathering data, 56
Reference books, as source of topics, 8
Reference book, citation, 168
Reference materials, blending, 128–130
References. *See* Citations; MLA style; Works Cited
Refining a topic, 2–9
Relevance of a source, 72–78
Religion
  academic model, 81–82
  search engines, 41
Report, citing, 131, 177
  online, citation, 187
Reprint, citation, 177
Reproductions, citation, 197
Republished book, citation, 171
Required instances for citing a source, 67–68
Research journal, 3–4, **36–37**
Research paper, **102–109, 214–219**
  body of, 123
  conclusion of, 124